FREEDOM REALIZED

FINDING FREEDOM FROM HOMOSEXUALITY & LIVING A LIFE FREE FROM LABELS

STEPHEN H. BLACK

FOREWORD BY JOE DALLAS

FREEDOM REALIZED

FINDING FREEDOM FROM HOMOSEXUALITY & LIVING A LIFE FREE FROM LABELS

———————

STEPHEN H. BLACK

REDEMPTION PRESS

ISBN 13: 978-1-68314-493-9 (Paperback)
978-1-68314-534-9 (Hard Cover)
978-1-68314-494-6 (ePub)
978-1-68314-495-3 (Mobi)

Library of Congress Catalog Card Number: 2017954862

TABLE OF CONTENTS

FOREWORD BY JOE DALLAS

"*But hereof be assured, that all is not lawful nor just that is statute by civil laws; neither yet is everything sin before God, which ungodly persons allege to be treason.*"
—*John Knox*

TRUTH-TELLERS IN A TIME OF error are like rain-washed mornings after a week of heavy pollution: refreshing, clarifying, and so badly needed.

Stephen Black has been a truth-teller for as long as I have known him. Aside from the special affection I would feel for any co-laborer in this difficult field of ministry to people with sexual struggles, I have come to admire his clarity, consistency, and uncompromised positions over the years. In fact, I have often walked away from conversations with him saying to myself, "This guy's got so much to say. He needs to be more widely heard."

Therefore, *Freedom Realized* is to me an answer to prayer and a validation of what I have suspected for so long—if only Stephen would put into writing what he has learned and experienced, so many people would benefit. Now, thank God, they will.

This book addresses the subject of ministry to people who are attracted to the same sex, who've chosen not to yield to those attractions, and are living in obedience to Christ's call and biblical standards.

Black knows these issues all too well as he has successfully dealt with the struggle himself. He then ministered to others just like him for decades. As the Director of First Stone Ministries and as a prominent leader, first within the ranks of Exodus International and now with Restored Hope Network, he has worn the mantle of Mentor, Apologist, Evangelist, and Teacher. When such a man has something to say, we'd best stop and listen.

Readers of *Freedom Realized* will be glad they invested the time. In it, Stephen chronicles the tragic demise of Exodus International, a prominent, long-standing ministry. He explains how doctrinal compromise and seeking favor with the world helped dismantle a work he valiantly tried to protect. Those who have followed the Exodus story or witnessed its collapse and wondered how it all came about, will get an insider's perspective, complete with clear warnings about veering even slightly from biblical integrity; warnings any thriving ministry should take to heart.

However, the bulk of the book is devoted to the following three areas: survey results drawn from people who have benefitted from First Stone's services, illustrations of effective ministry approaches to homosexuality, and explanations of the kind of arguments and resistances we can expect when we seek to show truth and grace to same-sex-oriented people. (The chapter on Practical Answers is worth the cost of the book by itself!)

Pastors and ministry leaders need this book as do families with lesbian or gay loved ones and individuals who wrestle with the tough questions many—myself included—have wrestled with when they realize their sexual desires will, if indulged, take them outside God's will. In that sense, *Freedom Realized* speaks to any believer whose cravings for one thing contradict their beliefs and higher values. This a struggle to which any Christian can relate. Perhaps the greatest strength of this book is its adherence to biblical principles as the final authority.

Since, of course, this is about discipleship, Stephen writes like a disciple offering information and guidance to other disciples. His passion for the topic is unmistakable, coloring these chapters with compassion and genuine concern.

God grant that this receives the broad exposure and readership it deserves. Despite extraordinary trials and obstacles, Black has labored to produce a tool to equip all of us. In this way, he instructs us to extend the hand of fellowship as Barnabas did to the repentant Saul of Tarsus, towards those who desire to faithfully steward their bodies and their sexual responses.

We are indebted to Stephen for this contribution. I am proud to be a part of this project and to call him a colleague, and I'm blessed to call him a friend.

—Joe Dallas, Author and Speaker

DEDICATION

I dedicate this book to my dear friends, the courageous founders
of the Restored Hope Network:
Frank and Anita Worthen, Annette and Andrew Comiskey,
Anne Paulk, Dr. Robert Gagnon,
Dr. David Kyle Foster, and Michael Newman

and to the all other Restored Hope Network Ministry Directors,
who stood courageously against the perverted grace message of "gay
Christianity," which brought about the
demise and implosion of Exodus International.
**Our ministries matter and are needed today—
more now than ever before.**

ACKNOWLEDGEMENTS

To Jesus Christ—I Owe All

To my wife, Robin Black—

for enduring long with me and giving me my greatest gifts in life; our friendship, relationship, and
our beautiful children and grandchildren. I am so grateful for the radiant gift you are.
Thank you, Robin! I love you!

To the two "green men" of my spiritual formation:
Milton Green and Keith Green—

both taught me, "absolute surrender to Jesus Christ as Lord, or He isn't Savior"—
I am eternally grateful!

To John Ward, my first pastor. You taught me wisdom in both the fear and the extravagant love of God that compels me to this day! In your pastoral care, I experienced discipleship in living out these truths, along with a surrendered devotion to family and a hope of restoration for my broken heart. You taught me spiritual warfare my first month of salvation, and you had me engrave 2 Corinthians 10:3-5 into my soul. I am so grateful to both you and your wife, Pat, for your sacrificial love and pastoral oversight to this very day!

To **Brad Yarbrough**, my second pastor. You continued to believe in me and encouraged me to stay the course for all these years!

To **Jerry Wells**, my third pastor. You tenderly and affectionately prayed over me many times and revealed Jesus' love to me. You always gave wise counsel.

To **Scott Fisher**, who challenged me with the Word of God along with Milton Green and Keith Green. You encouraged me to be a missionary for the glory of God and affirmed the call of God on my life.

To **Geri McGhee**, who took me through many hours of inner-healing prayer and deliverance. Geri is a woman of God who was very patient with me, giving me godly counsel through thousands of Scripture verses in my first years of marriage.

To **Don Giles**, my dear friend for life, who always has a word of encouragement from God's Word.

To **David Smithers**, my dear friend, brother, and a mighty prayer warrior. We now see the results. We have labored many hours together before the Lord, making intercessions and petitions, and have longed hard together in prayer for revival in the church. I am forever grateful.

To **Kirk Maynord**, who always encouraged me, never gave up on me, and has always supported me. Kirk, my amazing friend for life, I appreciate you!

To **Phyllis McGraw**, a spiritual mother, who was my greatest maternal source of encouragement as a new convert. You offered hundreds of hours of wise counsel and challenge from God's Word.

To **Ron and Pat Moore**, spiritual parents who took me into their home during my first year of discipleship to provide a safe place for me to grow. Thank you for teaching me Isaiah 26:3 to help me deal with my temptations and fear.

To Steve and Linda Riddle, I love you both dearly. You brought me to Christ and you provided a safe place to grow and be mentored by your Christian witness in the first six months I walked with Jesus! I am forever grateful!

To John Cooper, Chairman of the Board of First Stone Ministries, who is a never-ending source of wisdom, counsel, genuine godly affection, love, accountability. You are another true friend for life.

To the FSM Board Members: Randy Rice and Bill Hays, whose continued support and accountability are eternally valuable!

To Jeff and Lezlie Janes, who gave me the opportunity to serve full-time on staff with First Stone Ministries in 1992.

To the amazing staff of First Stone Ministries, and the two staff members who have endured decades with me: **Joseph Thiessen**, Office Administrator, and **Laura Leigh Stanlake**, Director of Women's Ministries. Thank you forever!

To Keith Adams, who worked beside me for a short season but gave tremendously, especially the amazing hours of processing my grief the first six months after my Charity died. I am forever grateful.

Grateful to God for Spiritual Formation

I also acknowledge many other major spiritual formation leaders who have poured into my life as I have spent many hours listening and reading, beginning with many humble Catholic nuns in parochial school, who deposited the truth of eternity. I am so grateful for those who poured into my soul after my born-again experience. I wish to acknowledge and thank all the names above. All of you guided my spiritual foundation and gave me a thorough education in theology and church history. From the lives of the following saints: Francois Fenelon, John Wesley, A.W. Tozer, Charles Finney, C.H. Spurgeon,

George Whitefield, John Bunyan, Jonathan Edwards, George Muller, John Owen, Watchman Nee, Dietrich Bonhoeffer, Corrie Ten Boom, Hudson Taylor, Reese Howell, Derek Prince, David Wilkerson, Bob Phillips, Leonard Ravenhill, James Robison, Andrew Murray, G.D. Watson, Oswald Chambers, E.M. Bounds, William Grunall, Jesse Penn-Lewis, Mike Bickle, Johnny Duncan, John Piper, John Wimber, Andrew Comiskey, David K. Foster, Sy Rogers, Michael Brown, Robert A.J. Gagnon, Larry Crabb, Neill T. Anderson, June Hunt, Kay Arthur, and many other leaders in the Southern Baptist and Assembly of God Churches in Oklahoma.

Last but not least, I am very grateful to **Sam Storms**, my pastor at Bridgeway Church in Oklahoma City, who gave me wise counsel during the Exodus implosion, and who never ceases to teach me rich truths found in the Word of God.

A Special Thank You
To Those Who Contributed to the Book

with their twenty-plus years of ministry experience:

Jerry Armeli, Shirley Baskett, Andrew Comiskey, Joe Dallas, Dean Greer, Phillip Lee,

Michael Newman, Anne Paulk, Lee Preston, Dan Puumala, Bob Ragan, Laura Leigh Stanlake,

Jason Thompson, Jim Venice, Frank Worthen, David Kyle Foster

To Those Who Helped Edit this Book

Jonna High

Kristen Tucker

Peter LaBarbera

Laura Leigh Stanlake

The Terrific Editors and Staff at Redemption Press

You are all amazing, mighty men and women of God!

ENDORSEMENTS

"*I love this book the way I love Stephen Black. His voice is passionate and as pastoral as it is prophetic. Stephen wisely sets the tone for 'Freedom Realized' in the recent history of Exodus' demise; Black then applies the real Gospel of Jesus Christ to homosexuality. In spite of the topic's complexity, Stephen cuts a clear and narrow way up the middle of what has become a contentious topic. He also paves a way for caregivers by giving statistical evidence for the effectiveness of truthful pastoral care. I have yet to meet a man who bears as patiently and tenderly with strugglers as does Stephen. His embodiment of truth and grace is echoed by the solid voices he enlists at book's end to declare: Jesus makes willing, wounded hearts whole. Thank you Stephen for your significant contribution to this wholeness.*"

—Andrew Comiskey, M.Div.
Author and Speaker
Founder and Executive Director of Desert Stream Ministries
Kansas City, MO
www.desertstream.org

"*It's one thing to be delivered from homosexuality. It's another thing to become a powerful, passionate, and uncompromising witness for the Lord, but that's exactly who Stephen Black has become through the amazing grace of God. Here, in this very important volume, he debunks the myth of "gay Christianity," exposes the dangers of today's compromised gospel, and gives practical, hope-filled instructions to those struggling with same-sex attractions."*

—Michael L. Brown, Ph.D.,
Author of *"Can You Be Gay and Christian?"*
Host of *The Line of Fire* radio broadcast
www.askdrbrown.org

*"A powerful testimony peppered with practical plans for anyone who **has** struggled, **is** struggling, or **will** struggle with same-sex attraction. Stephen's life proves: There's help... there's hope... there's freedom!"*

—June Hunt
Founder, CEO, CSO (Chief Servant Officer)
Hope For The Heart
Author, *Counseling Through Your Bible Handbook*

"Truth! Refreshingly, Stephen Black doesn't have a politically correct bone in his body. He's also a "bottom line" believer, who deftly zeros in on the heart of an issue by carefully listening to the Holy Spirit in Scripture and through prayer. For those who have wearied of continuously going around the same mountain while experiencing little freedom from homosexual confusion, this book is a finely targeted, guided missile designed to put God back in the driver's seat. For it is only from that posture of faith and humble submission that believers can appropriate the power of the Cross for the destruction of Satan's schemes and the eternal transformation of the soul. I highly recommend this book."

—Dr. David Kyle Foster
Author of *"Sexual Healing—God's Plan for the Sanctification of Broken Lives"* and *"Love Hunger"*
Founder and Executive Director,
Mastering Life Ministries and Pure Passion Media
www.purepassion.us

"*Stephen Black is a courageous culture warrior and a prophetic pastoral encourager. For over 25 years he has overcome some of the most extreme circumstances of life by the grace of Jesus Christ as you will read in* Freedom Realized. Freedom Realized *reveals that there is true, transformative grace to overcome homosexuality and that real freedom can be found through a devoted relationship with Jesus Christ as Lord.*

And he has faced staggering pain and adversity. On the very day he took a bold, biblical and national stand against the deceptive message of so called "gay Christianity," he lost his daughter, Charity, to unexpected death. He entered into a season of unspeakable grief as both a dad and as a spiritual leader. Yet, Stephen stood strong with tenacity and courage. He continued standing despite the growing animosity directed towards those who once proclaim freedom from homosexuality. He has endured a great test! Stephen is a testimony of God's freedom realized in the midst of great testing.

—Jim Garlow, Senior Pastor
Skyline Church, La Mesa, CA
Author of several books, the latest: *Well Versed—
Biblical Answers to Today's Tough Issues*
www.jimgarlow.com and www.skylinechurch.org

"*I have known Stephen Black personally for many years. Never have I known anyone with more passion for Christ and His Word. Never have I known anyone who walked the walk with more grace than this man of God. Stephen knows that truth—God's Truth—sets men free. His amazing new book, Freedom Realized, is a tangible display of God's truth that exposes the lies of the enemy and shows us not only that true freedom is possible, but that it is being lived out daily in the lives of people around the world! Change IS possible! Freedom IS being realized - regardless and in spite of what the popular culture would have us believe! This book is for anyone who dares believe freedom and change through faith in Jesus Christ is possible—and it is for those who still have doubt. The 'truth' of man leads to bondage. The*

Truth of God sets us free. Freedom Realized shows us the difference. I highly recommend this book to church leadership and laity alike."

—Dennis Jernigan
Author of *Renewing Your Mind: Identity and the Matter of Choice*
Founder and President of Shepherd's Heart Music
World-Renown Psalmist and Worship Leader
www.dennisjernign.com

"I am so thankful that God put Stephen Black in my life. Stephen is a passionate Truth Warrior. In an age when even Christian leaders cut spiritual corners to please men, Stephen preaches mercy, divine justice and the call to righteous living. No one can doubt his love for the homosexual struggler, nor his commitment to the Word of God (even the politically incorrect parts). 'Freedom Realized' offers solid evidence that people caught up in homosexuality, like all sinners, can overcome and lead godly lives through Jesus Christ. He eviscerates the shallow theology and false love of the "gay Christian" movement. This important book, like Stephen's own life, shatters one of the Big Lies of our age: that homosexuality is "who you are" and certain people's unchangeable destiny. It is a must-read for anyone who seeks freedom or desires to minister God's pure love to sexual sinners."

—Peter LaBarbera
President, Americans For Truth About Homosexuality
www.AmericansForTruth.org

"When Exodus International closed its doors in 2013, an opportunity arose for the world to see what real, transformational ministry to the sexually broken looks like. With over 20 years of data, Freedom Realized does just that! It's a rare phenomenon for Christian ministries to be so vulnerable and transparent as First Stone Ministries has in this groundbreaking book. In Freedom Realized, Rev. Stephen Black not only shows his raw emotions and vision for ministry to the sexually broken, but also, the raw data and numbers for what works and what does not in ministry. Freedom Realized

destroys the myth that "99.9% of homosexual strugglers do not change" by providing real feedback and data from nearly 200 ministry participants. But more importantly than the data is Rev. Black's first-hand account of how he and a handful of committed, courageous "Truth-Squad" warriors stood up to the heresy of Alan Chambers and his sloppy grace mentality for sexuality. In a compelling personal narrative, Black sets the record straight not only of the truth of transformational ministry to the sexually broken, but also, to the eternal truth that Jesus Christ saves, transforms, and changes—yesterday, today, and forever—those who earnestly seek His healing power. In Freedom Realized, we get an up-close view of how this practically works with Christ's humble servants. This resource is a treasure for all counselors, churches, and leaders of transformational ministries seeking to provide hope and wholeness to the brokenhearted!"

—Christopher Doyle, MA, LPC, LCPC
Executive Director, Institute for Healthy Families
Co-Coordinator, National Task Force for Therapy Equality
www.instituteforhealthyfamilies.org and www.equalityandjusticeforall.org

"Stephen Black's book provides a valuable piece of research from within his ministry sphere. He has captured views from a longitudinal, retrospective view on the validity of transformation. Today there is a growing disbelief that no one ever experiences a change in sexual preference. However, the results in this book concur with other recent studies. The reality is that many people do experience change. As Christians, we need to allow for the workings and the power of God and many can testify to his ability to transform lives, or to help us to master those things that once held us in the slavery of sin. Stephen lays out some key ways that the church can help people on this journey. This is a refreshing book for our confused times, with practical advice, blended with both truth and grace."

—Shirley Baskett
Director, Renew Ministries, Melbourne, Australia
www.renewministries.com.au

"Stephen Black has written a must-read book in light of the confusion created by former leaders of the now defunct Exodus International. Stephen's deep love for Christ, passion for truth, and personal involvement in redemptive ministries gives definitive credibility to this much-needed book on true and lasting freedom."

"Although deeply rewarding, serving in the area of sexual redemption can be intensely challenging. Stephen Black is one of the few ministers who walk faithfully and courageously in the Lord, in spite of lies from the enemy, animosity from the world, and misguided accusations from the 'progressive' church. Stephen's personal involvement in Exodus International (before it lost its way) give definitive credibility to this much-needed book on true and lasting freedom."

—Jason Thompson, Executive Director
Author of *Taking Back Ground and the online discipleship program*
Portland Fellowship, Portland, OR
Portlandfellowship.com

"In the ongoing culture war, Stephen Black is a true warrior, one who loves people enough to tell the truth about homosexuality. He's genuine and compassionate, and his gratitude for God's redeeming love in his own life is abundantly evident in his book, Freedom Realized.

This book brings a refreshing and much-needed message about God's amazing power to heal sexual brokenness. I highly recommend Freedom Realized, a book that will help readers see the power of God's redemptive work in action."

—Denise Shick, Executive Director
Help 4 Families—Ashland, KY
www.help4families.org
Living Stones Ministries—Glendora, CA
www.livingstonesministries.org

PREFACE / INTRODUCTION–WHY FREEDOM REALIZED?

"Those who do not learn from history are doomed to repeat it."
– George Santayana

Some History Explaining—"Why This Book?"

IN THE MIDDLE OF THE 1990s, I was hoping to compile a practical ministry guide for overcoming homosexuality and staying free. This occurred after my radical salvation experience with Jesus Christ in February of 1983 and was followed by eight years of preparation. At that point, I was in full-time ministry with First Stone Ministries in Oklahoma City. I had found lasting freedom from homosexuality and wanted others to experience it as well. I wanted to make a difference. Many books were being written, and one that caught my attention at that time due to its thoroughness was David Kyle Foster's *Sexual Healing—God's Plan for the Sanctification of Broken Lives*. I thought, "This book has everything I wanted to say and more; therefore, I don't need to write a book. Doing so would only feed pride."

Nevertheless, my hope to create a resource for those seeking freedom and those who ministered to them was rekindled. I have been called by my heavenly Father to comfort people with the same comfort I received in coming out of homosexuality in 1983. *Freedom Realized* is my obedience to that call.[1] I will share more about my story in the pages to come.

In the last ten years, there has been an increasing attack on the gospel-centered message of freedom from homosexuality. There are those involved in this cause who refer to themselves as "gay Christians." They are distorted grace advocates who contort what it means to walk in freedom in the church. These distorted grace advocates allow for these so-called believers in Christ to embrace a mental agreement on the historical facts of Jesus Christ while living unrepentant lives. They emphatically call these people both Christians and gay. They teach that you merely have to believe with no continued confession or repentance necessary. I have been surprised by some of these sources that promote the melding of Christianity with being gay. They wrongfully claim that being gay is a legitimate human orientation of sexuality and acceptable before God. Intelligent people point to their education and higher learning as preeminent over the principles and sound promises of God's Word, which is idolatry. You will find more on the topic of "gay Christianity" later in this book.

All that said, the real push to write *Freedom Realized* came from the Holy Spirit moving in my heart after the manifestly failed leadership of Exodus International from 2010 through the 2013 collapse.[2] I believe God wanted me to show firstly to the church and secondly to the world, *real* results to counter the distortions and lies coming from Alan Chambers (former President of Exodus International) and Clark Whitten (former Chairman of the Exodus Board of Directors). As sincerely as Alan communicates, he is wrong from a biblically orthodox view of grace and human sexuality. *Freedom Realized* is written to give hope and assurance of the transformative power of Jesus Christ. There is a sure hope that one can enjoy freedom from driving homosexual temptation and the pounding desires of same-sex lust, which many call same-sex attraction.

God's Word is forever settled in heaven! Grace is amazing and trans-formative-power, grace is abundant in mercy. Yet, grace requires a soul to walk out a lifestyle of confession and repentance from sin in the pursuit of a clear conscience from sexual immorality. Titus 2:11-14 (NKJV) and 1 Thessalonians 4:1-8 make this clear. God's grace provides the power for the truly born-again, sincere believer to follow Jesus Christ as Lord. Clark Whitten's teaching of

> *Freedom Realized* is writ-ten to give hope and assur-ance of the transformative power of Jesus Christ. There is a sure hope that one can enjoy freedom from driving homosexual temptation and the pounding desires of same-sex lust, which many call same-sex attraction.

"Pure Grace"[3] is keeping souls in bondage to sin through a false message of peace. His message is, "Don't worry about judgment." The fruit of Whitten's involvement with Exodus' staff and network are the many who have returned to embrace gay identities and are living as homosexuals.

This is truly tragic![4] They have Clark Whitten to thank for his pastoral care of Alan Chambers (former President) and Randy Thomas (former Vice-President) of Exodus. Chambers, an LGBTQ+ advocate, and Thomas, a gay man, are now both activists. Thomas has communicated in social media that he is proud to have meetings with the Human Rights Campaign and the Southern Poverty Law Center.

> Yet, grace requires a soul to walk out a lifestyle of confession and repentance from sin in the pursuit of a clear conscience from sexual immorality. Titus 2:11-14 (NKJV) and 1 Thessalonians 4:1-8 make this clear.

I started to become somewhat alarmed in 2006 when Clark Whitten, Chairman of the Board of Directors of Exodus, and Pastor Alan Chambers, began to teach in several Exodus leadership meetings. Alan invited his pastor to teach his, "reality of pure grace" doctrine. In 2008, I became alarmed, along with several other leaders, when I heard Whitten say, "You people, grace is so good that if you all want to go out to Ashville and 'lasciviousness' all over yourselves tonight, you can! Grace is that good!"[5] Whitten mocked and joked about the word *lasciviousness*. I remember feeling sickened as this was taught to all the delegates in a plenary session of the conference on that morning in mid-July of 2008. I remember the Holy Spirit reminding me of Jude 1:4, *"For certain men have crept in unnoticed, who long ago were marked out for this condemnation, ungodly men, who turn the grace of our God into lasciviousness and deny the only Lord God and our Lord Jesus Christ." (KJV/NKJV).* This was such a tragic turn for such a thriving network of ministries as Exodus had been! Founded in 1976, with Frank Worthen as the main leader, Exodus received its true doctrinal charter in the early 80s. It was a charter with a clear, biblically orthodox offering of hope for freedom from a life controlled by homosexuality. This is when Exodus really grew. One of the original proclamations of Exodus was, *"Freedom from homosexuality, not a method, but a person, Jesus Christ,"* which continues to be used by several ministries to this very day. At its peak, Exodus was a network of over 100 independent, para-church organizations. The network offered pastoral care, counseling, mentoring, support groups, resources, leadership training, teaching, church networking, and public speaking. Unfortunately, Alan Chambers and Clark Whitten decided that Exodus should no longer exist. Instead, Chambers later apologized to the LGBTQ+ community for the ministries of Exodus and how Exodus ministries calling for the repentance of homosexuality was harmful. Chambers turned upside down in his beliefs thanks to the mentorship of Whitten and his perverted "pure grace" teachings.

In Irvine, California in 2010, Whitten began to teach in a leadership meeting that 1 John 1:9, "was not written to Christians." It reads: *"If we confess our sins, he is faithful and just and will forgive us our sins and purify us from all unrighteousness."* He told the Exodus leadership that they no longer needed to be concerned about confessing sin, stating it was a waste of time because we were no longer under condemnation. *(You can plainly read this in his own book.)*[3]

In 2011, my internal alarm increased over the plan by the President of Exodus International, himself, to proclaim this heresy. Alan's pastor sharing distorted teachings was one thing, but now the leader of Exodus was going to do the same. Chambers embraced Whitten's distorted teachings and first announced this to the world on the Oprah Winfrey Network (OWN). On the Lisa Ling show in March of 2011, he stated that a person could be a practicing homosexual and go to heaven. I was personally and immediately concerned, having invested over twenty years with Exodus. I was truly devoted to Exodus by virtue of the fact that First Stone Ministries was one of the founding ministries of Exodus in 1976. In 2008, I was nominated to serve on the Ministry Council by Alan Chambers. I had previously made known my grave concern regarding Alan's leadership to the board members and the ministry counsel. Yet he and the board were systematically changing Exodus' bylaws. I personally believe that Alan's nomination of me to the council was a way to manipulate me. However, as events progressed, I became the Chairman of the Ministry Council in December of 2010 in order to serve. I took my role seriously—much more seriously than Alan realized. I aimed to bring protection to the network of ministries. This was the reason I remained with Exodus during this internal danger of increasing heresy.

Unfortunately, the positions and concerns presented by the Ministry Council were dismissed at the whims of its President, Alan Chambers. The Ministry Council was a volunteer group of ministry directors who tried to serve the network and who reported their concerns to the Board of Directors.[6] Initially, the Ministry Council was helpful for the health of the network. Unfortunately, the bylaws were changed and most appointees to the Ministry Council had no authority in the actual governance of Exodus International. With the bylaws changed, governing of Exodus changed as well, giving Alan Chambers more control. Clark Whitten was then empowered to promote his errant grace message. During the season from 2012 to 2013, the Exodus Board of Directors did not listen. They consistently replied to any concerns regarding the failed leadership of Alan Chambers with arrogant dismissiveness. Of course, the main communication from the board was from Chambers, Whitten, and Dr. Kathy Koch, Founder and President of Celebrate Kids. Later, I found out that some of the Board of Directors had not even been made aware of the grave concerns or hear what was being communicated on the Council's behalf.[6*]

Chambers continued his spiraling grace distortions on January 6, 2012. During a juvenile, frolicking appearance on the panel discussion with the "Gay Christian Network," Chambers proclaimed that virtually no one changes and that people really do not find freedom from homosexual desires or behavior. He said, "The majority of the people I've met, being 99.9 percent of them, have not experienced change."[7] Unfortunately, Alan continued his peculiar doctrinal spin and sowing of division into the body of Christ by his firm stand in his twisted beliefs. He descended further into deception by a compulsion to apologize to the LGBTQ+ community on national television. He did this once again on OWN with Lisa Ling, in 2013. In regard to the work of Exodus, he told the world that no one changes. He literally threw every former Exodus ministry, the very ministries that were supposed to be under his care, as well as the supportive church, under a bus of demonic heresy. The ridiculous part of this situation is that Chambers sincerely believes to this day that he is doing what is right. He actually believes he is being kind to homosexuals by rebuking the church.

Now, the secular media, the gay media, gay bloggers, the political gay-advocates, and the well-funded gang of bullies in the Human Rights Campaign and the Southern Poverty Law Center, use Alan's words over and over as some kind of authoritative statement. Alan's statement that, "No one changes," continues to be often quoted to indicate that no one really leaves homosexuality.

Some of the more mature leaders in the network of ministries of Exodus started seeing an erosion of theological soundness in 2009-2010 under the leadership of Clark Whitten, Alan's surrogate-father and emotionally enmeshed pastor. A few ministries departed. Most raised quiet concerns. These two men have brought about untold damage spiritually to thousands of people in the body of Christ. All who bring this to their attention are mocked as legalists. Anyone who does not agree with the Whitten and Chamber's message of "pure grace" (which is a perverted grace message of antinomianism[8]) is mocked as a Pharisee. Sadly, they have become heretical teachers of grace in an attempt to assure a segue to "gay Christianity," and communicate to the world that sound teachers of orthodox Christianity are legalists. This is truly an oxymoron.

Truth Squad!

In 2011, I was grieving. I did not really know what to do with what I was seeing in Exodus, so I started casually talking with other leaders to see if they had the same concerns theologically. I was depressed, and my heart was heavy. It was May 2011, while I helped with a Living Waters National Leadership training in Kansas. I could not stop thinking about Alan Chamber's appearance on "Pray the Gay Away?, *Our America*," with Lisa Ling, on March 8, 2011. He announced to the world that you can be a practicing homosexual and go to heaven in direct contradiction of many Scriptures.[9]

I was deeply concerned over the theological influence of Clark Whitten. I first sought out Andrew Comiskey, President of Desert Stream Ministries. With many tears, I shared my concerns with Andrew. I remember that day so clearly. It was during the Living Waters National Leadership training. We were outside, away from others, at a picnic table. Andrew communicated that he had not been following the dealings of Exodus, Chambers, or Whitten closely. He advised me to pray and see what might happen within the year. He also committed to start watching much more closely. I then tried to appeal to Alan about this theology during a Ministry Council meeting in June 2011. I had put together an agenda, and the last item addressed his proclamation that one can be a practicing homosexual and go to heaven. Alan saw the last agenda item and stood up, looked right at me, and said he had another meeting to attend. He did this with complete disregard to me as Chairman of the Ministry Council. Such was Alan Chambers' leadership style. Jeff Buchanan was also in the meeting and had concerns as well. I was grateful. Jeff assured me that it would be okay, that Exodus would not be transitioning to "gay Christianity."

It was a couple months later, at the end of the Summer 2011, when I called Frank Worthen. Many call Frank Worthen the "father of ex-gay ministry" as he was one of the founders of Exodus International in 1976. Frank was grieved over hearing what I told him, yet he was not surprised. He saw Chambers as a biblically illiterate, immature leader. In typical Frank Worthen kindness, he felt sorrowful for Alan. *"Poor Alan..."* Frank said. He calmly, yet with great authority, told me, "Stephen, you have no other choice, you must put together a Truth Squad! You must get together leadership and confront the Exodus Board and Alan." At this point, I had already appealed to Alan Chambers, Randy Thomas, Jeff Buchanan, and others to no avail. Chambers and

Thomas were predictably condescendingly dismissive. However, in Jeff Buchanan's defense, he was subject to Alan as his boss. Jeff was the only one in the Ministry Council meeting in June of 2011 who gave me any hope. Unfortunately, it became increasingly clear that this Exodus office leadership was not willing to listen to me. They were consistently dismissive of me for months. I remember thinking they might listen to a brilliant PhD on this subject, one who is respected as being a real authority worldwide. I had read some of Dr. Robert Gagnon's work and really liked it. A couple of years earlier, in the Summer of 2009, I had met Robert when he spoke at the Exodus Freedom Conference in Wheaton, Illinois. I begged him to have lunch with me. My thinking was that Robert could be a great asset to the future of Exodus. I was so grateful to meet and to confirm like-mindedness in theology during our lunch together. Understand beloved, Dr. Robert Gagnon is one of the world's experts concerning the theology and history of homosexuality.

Then, in November of 2011, I invited Dr. Gagnon to come to Oklahoma City to teach a weekend seminar from his amazing book, *The Bible and Homosexual Practice: Texts and Hermeneutics.* I confess, I had a hidden agenda! I explained to him all that had been transpiring and my deep concerns about what might happen to the Exodus network. I appealed to Robert Gagnon as the most scholarly man I knew. He had the authority, clarity, and courage to take on Chambers and Whitten. I appealed to Robert to watch carefully what Whitten and Chambers were teaching. To my eternal delight, he did. During this time, Alan Chambers was hurling off the rails of truth in social media posts and tweets. As a result, we watched Exodus derail to become a national train wreck. Robert Gagnon is one of my heroes in the faith as he became a constant blessing of living out Matthew 18:15-17 (If your brother sins against you, go and point out their fault...) Kindly, gently, and yet with great authority, Robert began to confront Alan and the Exodus Board, both privately and publicly. It was now almost weekly that distorted posts from Chambers appeared on Facebook and Twitter. Frank's Truth Squad was beginning to come together. Now, having known Robert for years, I consider him a dear friend who has an anointing like the Apostle Paul concerning the New Testament. He was greatly used as a part of Frank's Truth Squad!

January 6, 2012 saw a new shift of Alan Chambers as he continued his descent into antinomianism under the tutoring of Clark Whitten. He proclaimed his dishonorable (and now infamous) statement at the Gay Christian Network panel discussion, which was virtually no one really changes their sexual orientation. He stated he knew of very few and doubted those who had said they did change. This continues to be Chambers' claim to this day. It was becoming obvious that Chambers was living a conflicting reality of a gay man, married to a woman, and calling himself a Christian leader of an ex-gay ministry. He embraced and communicated the idea that he was in a mixed-orientation marriage with what he called, "Leslie desires" as his "orientation" for his wife.

It was two weeks later that the Exodus Member Ministries had an annual leadership meeting in Orlando. It was the first time in Exodus history where all leadership was required to sign a confidentiality form. The agreement demanded that nothing from the leadership meetings be repeated to anyone outside of the meetings. The atmosphere was controlling and oppressive, to say the least. It seemed that Chambers and Whitten were determined to "free" Exodus of directors, like myself, who confronted their unbiblical views. They had selected two board members, Clark Whitten and Mike Goeke, to sit at my table to "manage" me. Alan had preemptively sent me an email to warn me to be quiet about my disagreements. He warned me that I had better not be disruptive to his plans for the meetings, or I would be asked to leave. I was in shock. His plan was to re-market Exodus in his new way of thinking or to shut it down altogether. I was sick with grief over what was happening to Exodus. I was also angry. More than anything, I felt a dark, demonic force was trying to strangle me into quiet submission. I was also grieved by the leaders who were completely oblivious as to what was transpiring. My last hope was an appeal to a board member we thought was there to help us, Dr. Kathy Koch. Jim Venice, Keith Adams, and I spent several hours in talks with Dr. Koch in our hotel suite. To our heartbreak, instead of a help to us, she remained an ardent loyalist to Chambers, Whitten, and to their erroneous grace message. She even remained a board member throughout the implosion and oversaw the eventual closure of this once vibrant network. Dr. Koch can be seen on video proclaiming how supportive she was of the wonderful new grace message of Whitten.

It was this debacle of the heretical teaching and the dismissive leadership of Exodus that brought about Frank Worthen's Truth Squad. In my many conversations with Frank, we developed a list of people who might help. I remember calling David Kyle Foster, another hero in the faith. He was totally on board, having had some of his own regretful experiences with Alan Chambers. David Kyle Foster had previously seen the devastating error and began to confront Exodus. He had written an amazing letter of appeal to the board of directors, only to be dismissed by Whitten. Frank also suggested I call Anne Paulk. Anne was unaware of all that had transpired. I informed her of what she had missed. This took place after the Gay Christian Network circus. Anne was immediately on board. She was one of the Exodus board members who regretted hiring Alan Chambers in 2001. Anyone who knows Anne Paulk knows she is an amazing woman with many talents. Anne started her own investigation. She drove the ten hours to see Frank and Anita Worthen, and the Truth Squad was complete with Anne's skillful rallying. Not only was she on board, she went to work immediately to organize People Concerned for Exodus, a closed Facebook group made up of many directors of Exodus ministries who sought to discuss the issues that faced the network. I called several leaders to request their involvement. Anne and others had written letters of appeal to the board of directors, asking to removed Chambers. Then, on April 4, 2012, the entire leadership of Exodus' network of ministries received a response from the Exodus Board. In a letter written after receiving the results of a survey they produced for the member directors, they indicated they were unwilling to listen to our concerns. Instead, the Board made a unanimous decision to support and even empower Alan Chambers.

It became clear that a new, biblically-orthodox ex-gay ministry network would have to be formed. From the leadership group, People Concerned for Exodus, a vote was held to nominate the founders of the Restored Hope Network (Those names are listed in the Acknowledgements section of this book). What an amazing miracle! The Restored Hope Network came about quickly. We were organized as a 501c3 within months. This was truly miraculous given the hostile environment of the Obama administration. The first board of directors was voted on by all who attended the first gathering for the Restored Hope Network—about sixty ministry leaders—in Sacramento, California in September 2012. I have been so blessed to be a part of this amazing group of people. The valiant offering of the Restored Hope Network is largely due to the skillful leadership of Andrew Comiskey (Chairman), and Dr. Robert Gagnon, who has brought theological clarity. Because of these men and Anne Paulk, I have committed to continue serving the Restored Hope Network. I will do so as long as I am able. I am so grateful to God that Frank Worthen's Truth Squad was realized and produced this good fruit for him and Anita to see. I am also grateful that he was able to see the first five years of the Restored Hope Network's thriving in biblical truth and wholeness before he passed away on February 11, 2017. Frank will forever remain a dear friend and a hero in the faith to so many.

What the Devil Means for Evil, God Turns It for Good

The devil tries to harm maturing men and women of God by bringing sorrow, suffering, pain, betrayal, and great grief. We have the book of Job to understand this spiritual dynamic. These trials are allowed only through the approval of the Father. God, our Father, then turns it around in His economy, for those who love Him. The devil would like to destroy leaders; but, for those who embrace their destinies by dying to self and being conformed to God's plan, there will be victory! (Rom. 8:28-29) I do not think Anne Paulk, Andrew Comiskey, or I envisioned that 2011-2013 would be years of extreme pain. The Restored Hope Network was birthed during great adversity in all the founders' lives. Anne had experienced great betrayal and divorce. Andrew Comiskey also labored under the loss of ministry-related relationships in his unique betrayal. The others also experienced adversity. I was suffering as well and despondent at the shipwreck of Exodus and what it would mean for the church in America. At this same time, I was hit with the worst tragedy and grief when my adult daughter died suddenly.

Our heavenly Father truly used these years of great suffering to bring about deep bonding among the founders and increased conformity to Jesus Christ. We all embraced submission to the Holy One while in our great pain. We were accountable. We chose Jesus Christ and His cross-bearing ways over the sinful pleasures of the flesh and the world. God used this to birth His work in the Restored Hope Network, which is now a solid gift to the church. I am honored to walk with such holy and dedicated men and women of God across the entire network but especially with Anne Paulk and Andrew Comiskey.

Vision for the First Stone Ministries Effectiveness Survey

In April 2012, I believe the Lord reminded me of the more than 1,200 client folders of people who had participated with First Stone Ministries over our last twenty-five years. We heard Alan Chambers' bogus "99.9 percent don't change" claim as a continued mockery from gay activists. This was a dark time in my life. This was the very month my twenty-one-year-old daughter died. I was devastated, I needed a reason to move forward. I wanted other people to have hope. I needed hope! That is when an idea was born. *Why don't you find out just how effective First Stone has really been?* I believe this thought was from the Holy Spirit. It gave me hope as I worked alongside the Restored Hope Network founding board to combat Chambers' inspired mockery of freedom from homosexuality and to give truth that would *Restore Hope!* I decided to send out a survey to people in our ministry. This would reveal the effectiveness of not only our ministry, but other ministries that held to a biblically orthodox view—the mature ministries of Exodus that became the Restored Hope Network. This took three years to compile on a part-time basis with several wonderful volunteers such as Verla-Marie Hull. We converted all the First Stone Ministries' files into PDFs. My right-hand man in ministry, our office administrator, Joseph Thiessen, has amazing computer skills. Together, we developed a database. Finally, we built the survey with the aid of a statistician who gave his input and corrections to the survey. In November 2015, the FSM Effectiveness Survey was launched. The survey was completed in December 2016. We had over 1,030 email addresses. We were successful in contacting over 500 past participants. We closed the survey with 185 respondents. The rest is history! The remarkable results are displayed in a later chapter in this book.

> Our survey yielded more promising results than I had believed possible concerning the reality of change. The outcome revealed the truth that not only do people change, they find lasting freedom—thus this book, *Freedom Realized* came to be.

Our survey yielded more promising results than I had believed possible concerning the reality of change. The outcome revealed the truth that not only do people change, they find lasting freedom—thus this book, *Freedom Realized,* came to be.

The following pages reveal the statistical results of our survey. The results presented will contrast what does and does not work in finding freedom. By exploring my personal testimony as well as the testimonies of many leaders with over twenty years of experience, this book will show the hope-inspiring effectiveness of a forty-one-year-old para-church ministry. *Freedom Realized* is written to provide help to hurting souls as they seek to find the path to sure and lasting freedom from the bondage of sexual sin. Without a doubt, God's Word is true! Many people certainly find lasting freedom from homosexuality. They live free from a gay-identified lifestyle, despite what anyone else says!

Endnotes for Preface / Introduction

1. 2 Cor. 1:3-7 "Blessed be the God and Father of our Lord Jesus Christ, the Father of mercies and God of all comfort, who comforts us in all our tribulation, that we may be able to comfort those who are in any trouble, with the comfort with which we ourselves are comforted by God. For as the sufferings of Christ abound in us, so our consolation also abounds through Christ. Now if we are afflicted, it is for your consolation and salvation, which is effective for enduring the same sufferings which we also suffer. Or if we are comforted, it is for your consolation and salvation. And our hope for you is steadfast, because we know that as you are partakers of the sufferings, so also you will partake of the consolation."

2. Understanding of the demise of Exodus International—Several articles and links are located here: (http://www.firststone.org/articles/post/concerning-our-transition-from-exodus-international-to-restored-hope-network).

3. Critique of *Pure Grace* by Clark Whitten (http://www.stephenblack. org/blog/post/what-would-you-say-to-me-if-i-told-you-) and (http://www.stephenblack.org/blog/post/perverting-grace---red-flags-to-alert-you-to-perverse-grace-teachings/)

4. Ps. 119:89, Matt. 5:18, Heb. 13:8, Titus 2:11-14, 2 Cor. 3:18, Rom. 12:1-2, 2 Cor. 5:17, John 3:17-21

5. Christian Audio Tapes (www.catapes.com, Exodus08-D Grace, by Clark Whitten). Note: The quote referred to above regarding "lasciviousness" has been edited out of the recorded message. However, the laughing and mocking around the word *lasciviousness* on the audio does not make sense unless you had been there and heard Clark Whitten make this statement, which has been confirmed by several former Exodus leaders.

6. **2012 and 2013 Board of Directors of Exodus International consisted of the following:**
February 2011 board included Dennis Jernigan*, Ron Dennis*, and Jeff Winter.*
By June 2011 board had added John Warren* and Don & Diana Schmierer.
By October 2011 board had lost Ron Dennis* and Jeff Winter* and added Mike Goeke and Patrick Peyton.
By December 2011 board had added Kathy Koch.
(April 4, 2012, Exodus Board Letter sent out to network in complete support of Alan Chambers.)
By June 2012 board had lost Dennis Jernigan.*
By August 2012 board had lost Mike Goeke and Patrick Payton.
By March 2013 board had added Bob Ragan.*
By April 2013 board had lost Bob Ragan.*
By June 2013 board had added Tony Moore. The closing board of Exodus consisted of: Clark & Martha Whitten, Don & Diana Schmierer, Kathy Koch, and Tony Moore. This is the group that

empowered Alan Chambers through the heretical implosion and closure of Exodus International. The troubling constant was board chairman Clark Whitten about whose theology Dr. Robert A. Gagnon has repeatedly given warning. Whitten has been influencing Alan Chambers for over fifteen years as his pastor and the board chairman of Exodus. Chambers is the fruit of Whitten's oversight and ministry. Clark has referred to Alan "like a son." *= denotes board members not always aware of Clark Whitten and Alan Chambers' leadership decisions or communications. I would not be surprised after what other former board members have mentioned that only the closing board had a real indication that Chambers had embraced antinomianism. (See endnote 8 below)

7. Alan Chambers in his own words on YouTube video (www.tinyurl.com/in-alans-own-words) history (video found here: (www.tinyurl.com/in-alans-own-words-blog and http://www.stephenblack.org/blog/post/in-alan-chambers-own-words)).

8. **Antinomianism:** is a theological belief that Christians are under grace, and therefore, moral laws are of no use. This belief holds that God does not expect an obligation to obey the law. Christians merely need to have faith and believe. The word *antinomian* means: against the law, anti-law, or lawless. Antinomianism would be an extreme antonym of legalism. Many modern antinomians teach a perverted-grace or hyper-grace message where the Ten Commandments are not necessary and homosexual behavior is acceptable in so-called monogamous relationships. (Highly recommend Dr. Michael Brown's book: *Hyper-Grace*.)

9. Lev. 18:22-23, Lev. 20:13, Rom. 1:18-32, 1 Cor. 6:9-11, Eph. 5:1-17, Gal. 5:19-21, Jude 1:2-7, Rev. 21:8, Rev. 22:14-15

1

MY STORY—PART 1—HE SENT HIS WORD TO HEAL US

(First published in 1991)

"The law of the Lord *is perfect, converting the soul;
The testimony of the* Lord *is sure, making wise the simple..." Ps. 19:7*

*"He sent His word and healed them,
and delivered them from their destructions." Ps. 107:20*

I GAVE MY LIFE COMPLETELY to the Lord in 1983. As I did, He took me down memory lane as a part of my deliverance and lasting freedom from homosexuality. I remembered myself as a five-year-old little boy. I was curious about the male anatomy. This was the first remembrance of the beginnings of same-sex attraction. Many reason that curiosity about anatomy is an indication of orientation, but this is simply not true. The reality is that all little boys figure out that they are different than girls and natural curiosity is part of that.

At about age six, I was molested by a male babysitter, who was a friend of our family. This opened the doors to sexual distortions and clouded my mind with sexual uncleanness and perversion. The entrance of perversion in this way is typical of many I have pastored out of homosexuality. I was exposed to pornography at the same time in my development, which further distorted my understanding of sexuality. The pornography was heterosexual, yet was devastating to a healthy understanding of *real* love and God's design for sexuality. Examples of God's love is found in 1 Corinthians 13 and 1 John.

When I was seven, my brother's friends came over to our house to look at *Playboy* magazines. One of my brother's friends was reading an article about testing yourself to see if you might have homosexual tendencies. The article asked explicit questions to determine if you were attracted to men or women. My mind was reeling from the pictures and the feelings that I had. One of my brother's friends showed the pictures to me and asked, "Who would you kiss, the man or the woman?" Little did my brother's friends know that I had found and looked through their magazines beforehand. I became frightened about getting into trouble. I thought, "Well, we are all boys" (and seven-year-old boys are not supposed to be interested in girls), so I told him, "The man." With that, my brother's friends went on and on about how I was a queer. They ridiculed my brother and me.

I remember seeing my brother's face and how ashamed he was of me. I was greatly disillusioned and confused. I remember feeling so dirty, hearing their voices over and over saying, "You homosexual! You queer! You little faggot!" The voices of ridicule stayed in my mind and condemned for several days. I thought about human anatomy over and over in a state of confusion. These terrible scenes of injustice and cruel ridicule are typical experiences

> These terrible scenes of injustice and cruel ridicule are typical experiences of the many I have served over the many years of ministry.

of the many I have served over the many years of ministry. This exposure to pornography and ridicule is child abuse.

A few years later, when I was about nine years old, our next-door neighbors had some out-of-state friends visiting. I was playing croquet at their house in their backyard. I went into the garage, followed by the adult male visitor. He grabbed me from behind, my back resting tightly between his huge legs. He leaned down whispered into my ear as he began to molest me, "You know you wanted this. You know you wanted this." He would not let me go. He told me to be quiet. I was so scared. After struggling with him for a few minutes (which seemed like an hour), I finally got away. I was terrified at what had happened. I ran out of the garage and sat down like nothing had happened, yet I felt full of shame. His whispers were ringing in my ear. He blamed me for his own evil act of molestation. He came out of the garage and flipped me back in my chair and on to the ground, knocking the breath out of me. He looked down at me on the ground and said, "This is just a sample of what you'll get if you say anything to anyone." I was terrified! I went home and never told anyone. I felt such deep shame. I thought it was my fault because, in the heat of an Oklahoma summer, I was wearing cut-off shorts with no shirt. He had told me I brought on his molestation because I wore cut-off shorts. Looking back, I can see that the demons of hell were condemning me and placing a dark shame into my soul. I wonder how many other children do not realize they are victimized in this same way as abusers speak over them?

At about this same age, I received a book about witches from the parochial school I attended. This book contained chants and stories. I remember late one night, I began chanting out of the book. This chant was for power and acceptance. As I chanted, I began to feel a strong presence in the room. I became afraid and put the book away permanently. I was also exposed to fortune telling games for children. Since then, the Lord has shown me how the devil set up demonic control and further perverted my thinking through these experiences. I had given Satan ground in my life. All the voices I had heard were demons. These voices may seem like our own thoughts. The voices seem to be you talking to yourself. Remember though, not all thoughts that enter your mind are your own. According to the Scriptures, some may be demonic, "fiery missiles." (Eph. 6:10-18, 2 Cor. 10:3-5).

About a year later, my family went on a trip to Colorado. We stayed with friends of my parents. My parent's friends had a son who was a couple of years older than me. At bedtime, he had a "game" he had learned from another friend. He told me it was okay because it was just a game. I was molested again, except this time, I submitted to it because it was just a game. This was the time in my life when I began to learn about human sexuality. A year later, he came to visit at my house and we played the game again.

I now understand the reason the Lord reminded me of the things I experienced. It was to demonstrate that, though many people claim they are born gay, it is childhood influences and not genetics that incline one to homosexuality. Many say that they have had desires for the same-sex as long as they can remember. I was quite young when all this started in my life. I was exposed to sexual perversion and demonic influences at an early age. Yet, I had never really thought about all these episodes until the Lord reminded me of them after coming out of homosexuality.

> ...though many people claim they are born gay, it is childhood influences and not genetics that incline one to homosexuality.

I was one of those thousands of gay people who believed the lie that I was born gay. Homosexuality is a learned, sin behavior. In most cases, the behavior is inflicted by abusive outsiders then chosen as the lie takes root. These things can subtly creep into a child's life.

It is sad that my parents never knew what had happened to me. My parents loved me. Like most parents who love their children, they were brokenhearted to find out about these experiences. In my case, my parents' lack of knowledge of God and understanding of His ways resulted in my having no spiritual hedge of protection. (Job 1:10, 3:23). Though my parents made mistakes, they raised me the best they knew how. I don't fault them for my choices. The Bible says, "My people are destroyed for lack of knowledge. Because you have rejected knowledge, I also will reject you from being My priest. Since you have forgotten the law of your God, I also will forget your children." (Hosea 4:6 NASB).

The demons of hell had come to destroy my life without my parents ever realizing it. The sins of the forefathers are sins or desires that allow demonic influences to begin to manipulate even a small child. It is true that we are born with a sin nature (Gen. 3:7, 22). Babies are not taught to throw fits, become angry, or rebel; they do it all by themselves. It is also true that we inherit many traits from our parents. It is a scriptural principle that we inherit root sin habits and desires or the sins of the forefathers. However, this is not an excuse or reason to blame others for our own choices. We cannot blame our parents for our sins. We choose to rebel and walk in sin. It does not matter what the deception may be, it is our choice. We must take full responsibility for our choices, actions, and sins before a holy, righteous and just God. I have talked to people who have confessed their sins and the sins of their forefathers and received immediate measures of deliverance. It is important to confess and take authority over sin habits. (Neh. 9:2, Ex. 20:5 & Deut. 5:9-10, Prov. 28:13, 1 John 1:9, James 5:16). "For we are not fighting against people made of flesh and blood, but against (ruling) persons without bodies—the evil rulers of the unseen world, (against the spiritual forces of wickedness in the heavenly places), those mighty satanic beings and great evil princes of darkness who rule this world; and against huge numbers of wicked spirits in the spirit world." (Eph. 6:12 TLB & NKJV; Eph. 2:1-5).

When I was twelve, my family moved to another house. I attended a public school. Previously, I had attended Catholic school. I was in the seventh grade; I was introduced to drugs. I started smoking marijuana and listened to hard rock music and had the kind of friends who were always pushing for more and more sin. This was a sad time in my life. It was the beginning of a terrible year. I totally rejected what little I knew of God. This opened the door for a constant influence of demonic activity in my life; I became sexually active with a girl I met in school. I surrounded myself with peers who encouraged me to continue in sin. "Do not be deceived, evil companionships corrupt good morals." (1 Cor. 15:33 ASV).

After living this way for a year and a half, I became deeply depressed. I struggled with homosexual thoughts, desires, and dreams. I had given myself over to the desires of my flesh. I was so depressed that I would not talk to any of my friends. I remained this way for about a month. My family and friends became concerned. They constantly asked me to talk, but I would not. I was afraid of what everyone would think. At this point, I fully believed that I was homosexual. One night in my depression, I started praying to God to change me. I believed the lie that I was born gay. I tried to have a heterosexual relationship but could not stop the homosexual thoughts. I blamed God for making me gay. In great anger, I told God to change me, but I saw no change.

For the wrath of God is revealed from heaven against all ungodliness and unrighteousness of men, who suppress the truth in unrighteousness, because that which is known about God is evident within them; for God made it evident to them. For since the creation of the world His invisible attributes, His eternal power and divine nature, have been clearly seen, being understood through what has been made, so that they are without excuse. For even though they knew God, they did not honor Him as God, or give thanks; but they became futile in their speculations, and their foolish heart was darkened. Professing to be wise, they became fools, (Rom. 1:18-22).

This passage of Scripture paints an accurate picture of the life I was living. I had suppressed the truth of God for a lie. It was my fault, for even nature proclaimed to me that God was real and that my desires were unnatural. I did not honor God, nor did I give Him thanks, so my heart became darkened. Truly, I became a fool. *And with all deceit of unrighteousness in those who perish, because they did not receive the love of the truth, so that they might be saved (set free). And for this cause God shall send them strong delusion, that they should believe a lie, so that all those who do not believe the truth, but delight in unrighteousness, might be condemned. (2 Thess. 2:10-12).*

These passages of Scripture described perfectly where I was in my homosexuality.

I had another experience that caused me to believe the lie. There was a bully in one of my classes who ridiculed me *every day* by calling me "faggot." I became increasingly depressed. He picked up on my brokenness and my inability to relate to men and other male peers. I lost my bearings and starting to become more effeminate in my actions. I was so wounded and embarrassed by several bullies this boy had gathered. Their barrage of words were like arrows that sank deep into my soul. One day, some of these bullies followed me home from school. I ran up on a neighbor's porch, hoping they would think I was home. Instead, they charged me up on the porch, beating me, punching me in the face, and kicking me as I fell to the ground. "Black, you sissy! You faggot! You faggot! YOU FAGGOT!" As they screamed, they repeatedly punched and kicked me. When I finally arrived home, my dad (a Navy boxer), only said, "Well, I hope they look worse than you do." More shame… I was enraged! I was embittered, and a deep hatred grew in my heart towards my dad. It was a dark day in my life.

Remember the saying, "Sticks and stones may break my bones, but words will never hurt me?" Words do hurt, deeply. (Prov. 25:18, Ps. 52:2, Ps. 55:21). Satan's desire is to communicate rejection in all things. His wiles bring the rejection of self and pervert God's creation.

After all I had experienced, I decided to kill myself. The depression was too much. I was a queer, a misfit, a faggot! I knew nothing of communities of gay people. I only knew I was a misfit before God. I believe I would have succeeded in killing myself if it had not been for a "friend" who came over that very night. I was headed out the front door when he entered the driveway. He asked me, "Where are you going?" I blurted out, "To kill myself!" He said, "Oh! Come inside. I need to talk to you. I know what's wrong with you." I did not believe him, but I wanted to know what he thought, so we went back inside. We went to my room, where he told me that he thought my problem was not anything to worry about. He told me he was bisexual, and it was perfectly normal. I was shocked! A false peace came over me. One of my closest friends understood what I was felt. Then he seduced me and brought me into a new level of sexual perversion. Soon, I broke off my relationship with my girlfriend and pursued a relationship with him. This opened the door for my involvement in the homosexual community. Naively, in 1975, I did not know that there were other homosexuals. I was unaware that an entire section of society was homosexual—the hidden gay community of Oklahoma City. One thing led to another, and I went on to high school and met other friends. I went to gay bars and met other gay people. I thought all I wanted was to be "married" homosexually. Homosexuals joke about being "monogamish" and it is true. I knew of no homosexual couple that was faithful to one another.

A few years later, at my little sister's Catholic wedding, I talked with the priest who performed her ceremony. After the service, he said, "Stephen, I know why you have not been coming to mass." I asked, "Why?" He seductively glared at me and said, "It's all the more reason why you should." *(wink, wink).* About this time, my friends walked up, and we left. I thought, "He had to be gay." I was shocked! The priest just made a pass at me, yet this experience reinforced my false sense of peace. It gave me a great hope that the earlier conviction and guilt I had felt was not valid. I pursued gay-type "marriage" relationships with several men with various backgrounds.

I had one relationship that lasted two years with a wealthy older man named, Mike. I was nineteen years old. During that time, I was highly religious and returned to the Catholic Church. I attended college and was open with my gay life. I lived in a beautiful home with Mike. I drove a new, red Fiat convertible and had lots of money. I traveled and saw many places. I was worldly. I lusted after riches, and I thought that I was something special. (Rom. 12:3, 1 Cor. 8:2) A high school friend, Kim, had heard the reason for the break-up with my girlfriend. She mailed me a tract called, "The Gay Blade," produced by Jack Chick. It was so convicting. I showed it to Mike, and he told me to throw it in the trash. He said, "It's garbage." He thought he knew better because he was an elder in a prominent Episcopal Church in Oklahoma City. I threw the tract away but not without having thought about it for several days. I now understand how my heavenly Father was reaching out to me, to warn me of what was coming in the next few years.

Several months later, my little brother Christopher died suddenly from alcohol poisoning. We were only eighteen months apart in age. This was a major turning point in my life. For the first time in years, I began to pray earnestly. My mind became open to the fact that I would spend eternity somewhere. I cried out to God. I mostly complained to Him, for I felt *He* had taken my little brother. I tried to deal with my own appalling guilt, yet I was in deep grief.

At my little brother's funeral, I noticed that the same gay priest from my little sister's wedding was talking with Mike, the man with whom I was living. I thought it was strange, but it confirmed what I had thought earlier. Mike knew him well, and he knew many other gay priests and ministers in Oklahoma City. When I talked with this priest, he told me that being homosexual was okay with God. It was great because he led me to believe that God created us all this way. He said, "God loves us just the way we are." This ministered a false hope to me. At that point, more than ever, I believed that my homosexuality was preordained. Yet, I became depressed again for several months. I was filled with guilt about my relationship with my little brother. I was so convicted that I was worthy of death, I felt that I should have been the one to have died.

During this time of depression, my relationship with Mike ended in a horrible, alcohol-fueled fight. I joined a health club and met a new guy that I thought was straight. I will call him "Chase." He was a body builder, a lawyer, a top executive, and he helped me train. I was wrong about him. He had been exposed to homosexuality one other time earlier in his life. He was plagued with homosexual, lustful thoughts. One thing led to another, and I entered another relationship. However, he was married to a woman. Knowing this tore me up inside with guilt, and consequently, I developed an ulcer. Chase wanted to leave his wife and move to another state with me. He was a accomplished lawyer, well-connected, and could easily do this. As a Catholic, I knew this had to be wrong. I decided that I had to end the relationship. I could not stand the guilt anymore. I was torn up over this entire situation. (I know … strange morality.)

After the break-up with Chase, I decided to try to force myself to be heterosexual. I went into a relationship with a woman who just happened to want to try to help me out of homosexuality. My relationship with this beautiful woman, Melinda, was characterized by just as much sexual sin, lust, and guilt as all my other relationships. It failed to deliver me from homosexual lust. I still wanted to have a romantic and sexual relationship with a man. I did not realize that the real need I had could not be fulfilled in this way. My unmet needs from growing up needed an answer.

I can say now, after years of freedom, that my heavenly Father meets all my needs with many holy, God-affirming, affectionate, male relationships. Additionally, during the last years of my father's life, the Lord restored to me a wonderful relationship with him. I had felt so rejected and inadequate by my father. I had feared and rejected him back. Even so, I loved him dearly in his final days, and he was finally able to love me back. Even through rejection, we must turn our hearts to our fathers; otherwise, it will not go well with us. (Mal. 4:6, Ex. 20:12, Eph. 6:1-3).

In the final two years in homosexuality, I had been trained by other gay men to get the body into shape for the narcissistic worship of self! Going to the gym was a self-indulgent way to beef-up and be desirable. This was a typical part of the gay scene for me. I met a man named Steven at the gym, and I thought he was the perfect match for me. He was a champion gymnast and fed my perverted lusts! We hit it off great! Our relationship lasted for three months, ending the very day that I gave my life over to Jesus! After my conversion, this relationship was a real test for me. My relationship with Steven became a daily test after my conversion. Steven would call and cry over the phone, begging me to reconsider, claiming that real love would not do this. I was both immature in my handling of the situation and full of zeal for Jesus. I would now rebuke my ex-boyfriend and quote the Scriptures to him. Then, I shunned him. Subsequently, Steven turned on me and began to hate me as he communicated that I betrayed him for another, Jesus, my Savior and King. (1 Cor. 15:33, Prov. 14:16, 17:10, 18:6-7, 23:9, 26:4). Satan had played his last and best ploy of lust. I did not realize I was searching for holy love in a male relationship because all intimate male relating had been built in sexual perversion. It is impossible for members of the same sex to fix their broken identities through an inappropriate sexual relationship with another of their same sex. This is what homosexuals do not initially understand. You can never be completed by another human member of your same gender. I did not begin to understand the healing process until after I gave my life over to Jesus.

My Night of Deliverance

I was twenty-two years old at that point and had begun a transition from death to life. An old high school friend named Mary called me and said that we needed to go out on Saturday night since her birthday was on the following Monday. The next day, Sunday, February 6, 1983, Mary wanted to go see her sister. She warned me that her sister and her sister's husband were "real religious," but I did not care. We went to their house. I sat in their living room and listened to them tell Mary of God's ways. Mary's brother-in-law, Steve, and her sister, Linda, talked to Mary about Jesus in a way that I had never heard. They talked about Jesus doing this and that for them, answering their prayers. They talked about how Jesus would come and go from their home. I thought these people are crazy! I did not know of a Jesus like this! The Jesus I knew was dead on a cross and found in a wafer on Sundays.

Unexpectedly, the Holy Spirit spoke to me. (At the time, I did not know it was the Holy Spirit.) I heard this voice inside my head. It was the Lord, and He said to me, "If you do not accept Me tonight, you will die." My heart began to pound and pound. I knew that I had to know Jesus Christ like these people did. The ladies left the room, and I sat there with Steve. I said, "I need to know Jesus like you do." He jumped up out of his chair and said, "Well, brother I think the Lord Jesus Christ is calling you." I *knew* that was true. My heart was pounding. I had heard His voice! I prayed that night to receive Jesus Christ as Savior and LORD! I remember, as I prayed, I saw Jesus dying on the cross for me. I saw Him on the cross in a new way—alive and suffering for me. I believed in Christ. All my sin came out of my soul and into His body. What an amazing gift!

Steve led me in a prayer of surrender to the lordship of Jesus Christ. I felt the burden of sin lift! A few minutes later, the ladies came back into the room, and Steve told Mary that I had just been saved. Mary was unsure. She asked, "Did you?" I said, "Yes … um, I think so." Confused, I did not fully understand what all had happened to me. I was overwhelmed, and I

> I remember, as I prayed, I saw Jesus dying on the cross for me. I saw Him on the cross in a new way—alive and suffering for me. I believed in Christ. All my sin came out of my soul and into His body. What an amazing gift!

did not understand the terminology, "being saved." On the way home, Mary asked me, "Well, does this mean you're not going to be gay any more?" I said, "Hmmm, I don't know, I guess it means whatever Jesus has for me."

Later that night, after arriving home, I went to my bedroom with the old, unused family table Bible. I began to pray for God to show me whether my homosexual lifestyle was wrong. I wanted God to show me from the Bible if homosexuality was right or wrong. My parents owned a massive Bible from the Vatican with many extra pages and pictures. I did not know where to start. I flipped opened the Bible and landed on Leviticus, chapter 18. I noticed a paragraph header on "Laws on Sexual Immorality" and my eyes fell

> On the way home, Mary asked me, "Well, does this mean you're not going to be gay any more?" I said, "Hmmm, I don't know, I guess it means whatever Jesus has for me."

upon verse 22. It was a miracle from God! "You shall not lie with a male as one lies with a female, it is an abomination." Lev. 18:22 (Lev. 20:13). Of all the places I could have flipped open the Bible, I flipped open to Leviticus 18. God had ministered His law to me, so I could see my need for Jesus Christ. (Gal. 3:22-24, Rom. 7:7, Matt. 5:17-20).

I did not know what "abomination" meant. By looking at the word, I knew it had to mean something that God really hated. I knelt beside my bed and cried out to God for forgiveness. I prayed, trusting Jesus Christ to totally change my life. From that day, I have been totally transformed. I am not saying I did not have to work through a lot because I did! As a matter of fact, for the next year, I came under all kinds of temptations and trials. What was miraculous and amazing was that I was able to immediately stop acting out sexually! This was truly a miracle as I was a sex addict! After my conversion, the next several days were filled with great conviction over all my sin. I faced multiple demonic attacks. I confessed my sin to Steve, and he prayed with me again and again. (James 5:16). I began to search for a church. The Holy Spirit led me to a group of people who loved God with all their hearts and who worshiped in a building in the shape of a tee-pee!

I found out later that the believers at this fellowship had been praying for my salvation during a Bible study. Thank God for those who pray and believe God for souls! If you pray for someone, don't ever stop! Keep praying! It is a crucial step to find a group of people who with whom you can fellowship and who can encourage you and hold you accountable. Pray and ask Jesus to help you find the right place. He was faithful to me, and He will be faithful to you, for God is not a respecter of persons. (Acts 10:34, 35).

Deliverance from homosexuality comes only from Jesus Christ. It does not come from great counselors and ministries. Certainly, God does use these people, and I would advise to seek as much help in counseling and therapy as is necessary, but you must realize that true freedom comes from Jesus Christ and Him only. Total deliverance from homosexuality comes only through a new lifestyle of absolute surrender and a complete dependence upon Jesus Christ as Lord.

> Total deliverance from homosexuality comes only through a new lifestyle of absolute surrender and a complete dependence upon Jesus Christ as Lord.

We must demonstrate our belief in Jesus through genuine repentance. We must believe His promises and stand on the Word of God and determine to obey Him. Ask Him to help you. The axe must be laid to every root of sin in our lives in order that we walk fully with Jesus. This is where counseling, pastoral care, and therapy may help. I had a deliverance minister assist me with my great pain and inner healing. Unforgiveness and bitterness are major root problems. Many homosexuals are hurting, bitter people because they have been grossly sinned against. This is partly because many had a very poor relationship with their own earthly fathers. For most, they have never experienced true masculine love and have not experienced the Father heart of God. People in homosexuality view their relationship with God the Father similarly to how they view their relationship with their earthly fathers. They reject God in anger and bitterness. Legitimate need for father-love is diverted into sexual expressions often because of the trauma of their own sexual abuse. We all need healthy love desperately, especially those involved in homosexuality. We should remember that real freedom from all sexual perversion and all forms of sodomy—of even the worst kind—comes only through faith in Jesus Christ. "Faith comes by hearing and hearing by the Word of Christ" (Rom. 10:17).

Jesus is the living Word. He is the powerful, transformative grace we need to overcome sin. The grace of God in Christ Jesus, our Lord, is sufficient for us in our weakness. The humble receive grace. Therefore, we must humble ourselves daily to receive His grace and His power daily. (James 4:6). "God will not be mocked, for whatsoever a man sows, this shall he also reap. For the one who sows to his own flesh shall from the flesh reap corruption, but the one who sows to the Spirit shall from the Spirit reap eternal life" (Gal. 6:7). This Spirit-sowing must be daily. Nature itself proclaims God's invisible attributes, His eternal power, and divine nature. (Rom. 1:20). God's way is for one man to be with one woman as a sexual complement for life. This is natural! (Gen. 1:26-27).

God made no mistakes when He created us anatomically. Human biology screams this fact! Make no mistake about it, God created the male and the female to live and work together emotionally, spiritually, and physically. *Blessed is a man who perseveres under trial; for once he has been approved, he will receive the crown of life, which the Lord has promised to those who love Him. Let no one say when he is tempted, 'I am being tempted by God,' for God cannot be tempted by evil, He Himself does not tempt anyone. But each one is tempted when he is carried away and enticed by his own lust. Then when lust has conceived, it gives birth to sin; and when sin is accomplished, it brings forth death. (James 1:12-15).* We must cry out to God for deliverance! According to His Word, God hears the prayers of the repentant and sees the heart of the person who is truly being honest with Him (Ps. 51:17).

Do not try to test God, but be totally honest with Him. Humble yourself before God, confess every sin and motive, and He will be gracious to you. His grace will bring power to overcome any sin. Hope in God for the rest of your life. Trust fully in Him, commit all your ways to Him, and He will surely make your steps straight. (Prov. 3:6, Ps. 37:5). I praise God every day for His deliverance from the dark pits of homosexuality. When the memories of the past surface, I just turn them into altars of praise to Him for His mighty deliverance. My goal is to continually worship Him in *every* trial and temptation.

I have written this history to give *hope* to others who might be reading this. I do not like to recall my former life. I wish I could erase the six perverse, sex-filled years of living as a gay man. I want others to know of the mighty deliverance of Jesus Christ. Many have accused me of not ever being gay, but that is as far from the truth as it could be. I lived completely gay-identified, and it was really dark! I am *no longer gay* since I came to Christ. Now, I rarely suffered from the haunting, same-sex attractions and lusts. Sure, the first years were difficult, but I continued to press into Christ and His community. My old self died in Jesus Christ, and I have a new life now because of His love at Calvary. I do not identify as gay or even ex-gay in any way in my internal thinking because I don't embrace labels.

We must constantly thank God for everything He does in our lives. My heavenly Father has given me a beautiful, merciful wife. We have been married now since May 25, 1986, and we have three beautiful children and three grandchildren. God's blessings never cease when we are open to Him in obedience.

Bible study notes of the truths in this first part of my story. The following verses are passages I have put to memory and meditation over the last thirty-five years.

Rev. 12:11, Prov. 9:10, Prov. 10:27, 14:27, 16:6, 19:23, Job 28:28 and Ps. 34:7-10 & 111:10 Rev. 14:6-7, Luke 24:47, Isa. 30:15, Heb. 4:14-16, 1 Cor. 10:12-13, James 4:6-10, Titus 2:11-12, Ps. 51:17 and 32:1-5, 1 John 1:9, James 5:16, John 1:1, 1 John 1:1, Rom. 10:17, Heb. 11:6, Ps. 119:105, Matt. 4:1-11, James 1:21-22, 1 Peter 1:23, Ps. 119:9-16, 2 Cor. 10:3-5, Eph. 4:23,1 Peter 1:13-16, 1 Peter 4:12-13, Eph. 6:10-18, 2 Cor. 5:17, Gen. 3:1-5, Rom. 1:25, Gal. 5:19-24, 1 Cor. 6:9-11, Eph. 5:5-6, Rev. 21:8, Ps. 68:5-6, Ps. 103:13, John 14:9-10, Rom. 8:31, Rom. 8:15, 1 John 4:8-11, Ps. 25:14, 2 Cor. 1:3-4, Mal.

4:6, Ex. 20:12, Eph. 6:1-3, Matt. 18:21-35, John 14:26, 1 John 2:27, 1 Peter 5:8-10.

2

OVERVIEW OF HOMOSEXUALITY

"Homosexuality is not normal. On the contrary it is a challenge to the norm. Nature exists whether academics like it or not. And in nature, procreation is the single relentless rule. That is the norm. Our sexual bodies were designed for reproduction. No one is born gay. The idea is ridiculous. Homosexuality is an adaptation, not an inborn trait."
—Lesbian activist and writer, Camille Paglia

"And such were some of you. (practicing homosexuals—vs. 9). But you were washed, you were sanctified, you were justified in the name of the Lord Jesus and by the Spirit of our God."
—1 Cor. 6:11

I SHARE THIS OVERVIEW OF homosexuality after the first part of my story since what I experienced demonstrates many of the points of causality that are typical for those who practice homosexuality. I want you, the reader, to have some understanding before looking at the survey results near the end of this book. It is important to gain perspective on what homosexuality is and the frequent root sources which are commonly dealt with by people who find freedom. I share my own personal perspective, and after completing and studying the research, I relay the causality derived from the study as well as many other professional counselors and therapists. I also have my own observations from three decades of helping others in ministry. You will also learn as you read the leadership submissions. Frank Worthen has offered this helpful, concise description of homosexuality:

"Homosexuality is a misguided search for love and affirmation in sexual behavior that is contrary to nature."

Contrary to nature indeed! St. Paul wrote to the church in Rome to describe homosexuality as a suppression of the truth and an embracing of unrighteousness. He went on to say that homosexuality is manifested as people rely on a distorted thought processes that exchange the natural attraction toward the opposite sex for a burning desire towards their own gender for sexual pleasure. In Romans, chapter 1, a clear judgment of God upon those who do not repent is that they are turned over to the consequences of their false belief. This should give you pause. God allows for people to believe lies and ultimately be damned.[1] Yet, today we have people in the church who read right over this passage and do not see what has already transpired. This same judgment is now falling on the land and in the church as many embrace homosexual practice as a God-affirmed alternative. They believe the lie that homosexuality is merely an alternative lifestyle based in psychology. It is frightening to see many in the church at large embrace the idea that same-sex attraction and a gay identity are a legitimate part of human relating. They embrace this position out of their own confusion about human sexuality and God's divine intent. When I hear that kind of communication, it immediately sends up a red flag. I feel concern regarding their worldview about sexuality in their own lives and the kind of behaviors they deem acceptable, but that is a topic for another book. For now, it is enough to say that when it comes to the state of the church, there is a rampant descent into sexual immorality, serial adultery, and pornography, the church must address all of these grievous sexual sins if we ever hope to help the homosexual. This hidden and rampant sin in church leadership and church members alike has caused great confusion in this generation, which in turn has fueled the normalization and acceptance of homosexuality.

Understanding Homosexuality

It is important to understand the common causes of homosexuality if we are to compassionately help anyone to recover. What follows are described causalities. This list is not necessarily complete. It is an outline, but it is thorough. The list will not be given with great detail in this book. This chapter is merely an *overview* of homosexuality. It will be helpful to keep things simple. Herein we begin with causalities then move on to the list of points of pastoral care that I consistently address to help people find lasting freedom. For further understanding of homosexuality, I suggest reading Joe Dallas' *Desires in Conflict*, Joseph Nicolosi's *Reparative Therapy of Male Homosexuality* and *Healing Homosexuality: Case Stories of Reparative Therapy*, *Hope for the Same-Sex Attracted*, by Ron Citlau, and the *Such Were Some of You*, documentary by David Kyle Foster. There are many other books and videos found in the Resource chapter of this book. Now for the overview points I typically use to help in ministering:

> It is important to understand the common causes of homosexuality if we are to compassionately help anyone to recover.

Homosexuality Begins in Childhood

We begin with the belief that most who struggle with same-sex attraction do not make the choice to be same-sex attracted. Homosexuality typically begins with same-sex attractions that start early in life. Most agree on this issue. But the question is, why? Is there something going on in early childhood that should be explored? I think so. It certainly was the case with my own history and the histories of several hundred men I have personally spent time with in pastoral care. The development of a person's temperament, the way they view themselves, and their own perceptions can often cause insecurity in the development of their identity.

Some Common Causes of Homosexual Development
Temperaments / Personality / Gifting / Interests—Perceptions

- **Early Childhood Development**
  - ✓ Experiences—fear, insecurity, ridicule
  - ✓ Perceptions of One's Self—this is usually an area of great need of pastoral care.

- **Childhood Sexual Distortions**
  - ✓ Abuse, Pornography, Molestation, Exhibitionism—at least half of the people we have served in ministry have been sinned against by sexual abuse.
  - ✓ Seductions—verbal, and/or physical sexual abuse

- **Family Background**
  - ✓ Breakdown of the Family. Father-absence through divorce, death, or other circumstances can cause distorted versions of family. Children raised by homosexual parents or parents involved with multiple partners can greatly influence the early development and erode a sense of identity.
  - ✓ Sins of the Forefathers (see Ex. 20:5)

- **Peer Pressure**
  - ✓ New Social Acceptance—experimentation in homosexual behavior is encouraged, especially among young women. Lesbianism has been encouraged as a form of "friends with benefits" in order to discourage the fear of pregnancy and abortion.
  - ✓ Gang Activity—some gangs have perverse initiation rites for entry.

- **Prison Life**—many incarcerated in male prisons have been forced to engage in homosexual behavior. Rape is common. In female prisons, lesbianism is encouraged. We see evidence of this in slogans such as, "gay for the stay" and "two is better than one." This happens for the purpose of protection and comfort.

From my experience, these overall common causes were true for the majority of the men I have served in pastoral care. Most of the people we serve had at least some kind of sexual distortions in their childhood histories before puberty. This is a direct result of a culture that has lowered all sexual norms from a Christian, biblical worldview of morality. We now suffer the results of Alfred Kinsey's indoctrination[2] and also the degenerate influence of the pornography industry and Hollywood's low standards of acceptable sexual relationships. Together, they have made sexual immorality the norm and given rise to more homosexual activity and exposure.

Below are two diagrams I often use in teaching: *An Overview of Homosexuality* and *Common Causes to Homosexuality*. Upon closer scrutiny, you will see there is a consistent pattern of areas in need of pastoral care. If the areas shown are not fully processed in counseling, the likelihood of relapse and return to homosexuality is high. The reason First Stone Ministries has had such a high success rate is directly tied to our thoroughness in addressing these issues. This will be seen in the survey portion of this book.

Overview of the Common Causes of Homosexuality

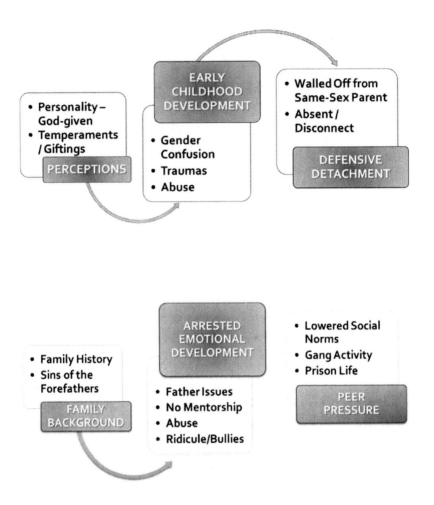

Common Causes Explained Further—Early Childhood Development

1. **Father Wound**
2. **Defensive Detachment**
   - ✓ Absent Father / Emotional Detachment
   - ✓ Hostile / Angry / Scared

✓ Rejection / Ambivalence
✓ Physical Abuse
✓ No Affirmation of Healthy Masculinity
✓ No Affection—Passive
✓ Arrested Emotional Development*
✓ Perceptions from Temperament*
✓ Bottom-line: They *feel* they just don't add up
* *Typical in most cases*

Defensive detachment occurs due to the thought patterns and emotions of an individual struggling with same-sex attraction. It manifests as building an emotional wall against the same-sex parent. This is common, and as you can see, there are many reasons this occurs. It is not always the parent's fault. Often, the perception of the struggler is what causes defensive detachment to take place. Insecurity, fear, and comparison are always present in people who struggle with homosexuality. The need to mentor gender development in a healthy environment is imperative for recovery.

Understanding Homosexuality—Common Cause Points in Need of Intense Care

Usually at least one year of pastoral care or counseling is required to address the following:

3. Lack of Mentorship—No Role Models
✓ Strong Feminizing Influences (males)
✓ Strong Masculinizing Influences (females)

4A. Mother Wound / Broken View of the Feminine
✓ Dominant Mother / Husbanding / "Girl-friending" Sons

- ✓ Femininity Unsafe—wounded mother in both males and females who struggle
  - Manipulation
  - Control
  - Gender Bashing
  - Broken Marriages

4B. Mother Wound / Broken View of the Feminine—Common in Female Homosexuality

- ✓ Family Dynamics
  - Mother-Daughter—relationship distorted
  - Father-Daughter—protection of femininity in his daughter is weak or not established
  - Parents' Marriage—a broken representation of healthy relating
- ✓ Peer Pressure
- ✓ Judgments and Inner Vows—perceptions of oneself, femininity is a vulnerability
- ✓ Gender Rejection
  - Flight from Mother
  - Judgments (internal confusion)
  - Feminism or Feministic Ideologies—Gender Distortion— perverse and unsafe cultural messaging
  - Negative and Harmful Experiences with Males—this is highly common in female strugglers. Most years, the majority of the women we minister to in pastoral care have been physically and/or sexually abused by men.

5. Sexual Distortions & Sexual Abuse

- ✓ Pornography & Exhibitionism—mental, emotional, and visual distortion
- ✓ Verbal Seduction—emotional distortion
- ✓ Sexual Abuse & Molestation
  - Incest & Rape
  - Our ministry experience reveals that the majority are wounded in their sexuality by others.

6. Environmental Factors' Effect on Temperament and Personality Traits

- ✓ No Touch or Care
- ✓ Rejection / Identity Conflict / Self-acceptance Issues
  - Deep-rooted rejection—RIDICULE = doubt and fear
- ✓ Identity Conflict / Self-Acceptance /Temperaments
  - Sensitivity / Artistic / Emotional (male strugglers)
  - Rough, Tough & Tumble (female strugglers)
    "He (she) is just so different." "He acts like a girl." "She acts like a boy."
- ✓ Arrested Emotional Development
- ✓ Identity Conflict and Confusion
  - Self Esteem—How you *feel* about yourself (psychology).
  - Self-Image—How you *see* yourself (mental picture).
  - Identity / Acceptance—"Who *you are in fact*" (biblical).

7. Adoption—Rejection / Identity Conflict / Self-Acceptance Issues

- ✓ Adoption = Rejection = Never good enough

8. Identity conflict and confusion through:
- ✓ **Peer pressure**
  - Gang activity
  - New social pressures (fads / Hollywood)
- ✓ **Prison Life**
  - Sexual perversions
    - » Forced
    - » Accepted

For Freedom to be Realized, There Must Be Counseling and Pastoral Care for the Following:

The following commitments or points of understanding must be present for freedom to be realized related to the common causes of homosexuality:

Freedom/Healing & Change Can Only Come When:
- ✓ One really wants to change
  - It is a **fight;** "a fight of faith"
- ✓ One must gain understanding of the whys of same-sex attraction
  - Your own history
  - Identify the conflicts and roots (receive ministry & counseling).
- ✓ Understand and embrace a process of change with a purpose

Pastoral Care and Counseling—Points to Address to Give Hope
- ✓ **The Roots –What lies behind the causes?**
  - Rejection / Self-Pity
  - Rejection / Self-Hatred
  - Anger—we must resolve anger and bitterness towards
    - » God

- » Family
- » Others—Self
- Bitterness
- A Spirit of Ungratefulness
- Rebellion / Fear
- Insecurity / Fear
- Envy—"cannibalism of soul"—inordinate attractions/desires/lust to consume another
- Pride and Narcissism—the false self / the love of self
- Gender Insecurity—Repair the loss of gender affirmation and gender identity
- Idolatry
- Emotional Idolatry/Emotional Dependency
- Moral Impurity—Sexual Addictions
- Spiritual Oppression / Warfare—Gain understanding and equip people to do battle with demonic forces. (Eph. 6:10-12, 1 Peter 5:8, John 10:10). There must be a sincere faith and belief that Ephesians 6:12 is applicable.

A Concise Conclusion. Homosexuality Is Rooted In:
- ✓ Deficits in the relationship with the same-sex parent
- ✓ Environmental Factors such as abuse of various kinds by family, peers; unhealthy relations
- ✓ Arrested Emotional Development—stuck in childhood emotional brokenness rather than maturing and developing as productive, healthy gendered adults. This is like the Peter-Pan mindset, yet in one's sexuality—the need for emotional connection is sexualized.
- ✓ Lack of Nurture, Not Nature (There is nothing scientifically that points to a genetic cause),[3] which creates a need for gender mentoring/development.

- In recovery from same-sex attraction, there is a great need to assist the person in recovery in the nurture and affirmation regarding one's gender and beautiful uniqueness.
✓ Distorted and confused perceptions and identity conflicts
✓ Homosexuality and same-sex attractions are unnatural desires and feelings that are a result of the sinful fall of humanity. Homosexuality or "gay Christianity" should never be recognized as a legitimate identity in the church or legitimate as an orientation; to do so only sows a cruel bondage of lowered sexual ethic for the next generation.

Concerning Freedom:
✓ Freedom is not the absence of a struggle.
✓ Freedom is the ability, by God's grace, to rise above darkness and a life controlled by anything, especially sexual immorality.
✓ Freedom is the continued walk of holiness with Jesus Christ as Lord.

Endnotes:
1. Rom. 1:21-27, 2 Thess. 2:10-12
2. For further reading, consider: *Stolen Honor—Stolen Innocence—How America was Betrayed by the Lies and Sexual Crimes of a Mad Scientist (Alfred*

> Homosexuality and same-sex attractions are unnatural desires and feelings that are a result of the sinful fall of humanity. Homosexuality or "gay Christianity" should never be recognized as a legitimate identity in the church or legitimate as an orientation, to do so only sows a cruel bondage of lowered sexual ethic for the next generation.

Kinsey) by Judith Reisman, Ph.D. (Orlando: New Revolution Publishers. 2013)

3. Charisma News: *Johns Hopkins Scientists Offer Absolute Proof Gay Agenda's 'Born This Way' Is a Lie,* by Brendan Bradley http://www.charismanews.com/world/59417-johns-hopkins-scientists-offer-absolute-proof-gay-agenda-s-born-this-way-is-a-lie *The New Atlantis—A Journal of Technology and Society—Special Report, Number 50—Fall 2016 Issue "Sexuality and Gender Findings from the Biology, Psychological, Social Sciences" by Dr. Lawrence S. Mayer, M.B., M.S., Ph.D. and Paul R. McHugh, MD*—http://www.the-newatlantis.com/docLib/20160819_TNA50SexualityandGender.pdf. This report conclusively reveals that there are no genetic links to homosexuality. No one is born gay. The American people have been lied to. (For more up-to-date information on, "No One Is Born Gay" go to my blog: www.stephenblack.org.)

3

MY STORY—PART 2

1999 to Present
The Healing Power of Pain—
The Crucible of Suffering Produces Life

"Do you not know that those who run in a race all run, but one receives the prize? Run in such a way that you may obtain it. And everyone who competes for the prize is temperate in all things. Now they do it to obtain a perishable crown, but we for an imperishable crown" —1 Cor. 9:24-25

I SHARE THIS NEXT PART of my story because the first part ends in such victory. It could seem that from the outside; I have been living a joyous life with no problems for these many years. Although homosexuality and same-sex attraction no longer nag at me anymore. I want you to know that my life has actually been one of a crucible with many other tests and trials of my faith. It seems as though a sincere Christian coming out of homosexuality might communicate that life is lived happily-ever-after. This would be disingenuous to the real Christian life and certainly not true of my story. I want the reader to understand it is not how you begin the race that matters but how you finish. There will be many trials, and many will fall away from a diligent faith unto the end. In fact, many already have. Beloved, for me the most trying years of my entire life have been the later years. I want to share with young Christians here, it is very important to know, we are all called to endure and be faithful to the end.[1]

Several years ago, I had a half-day intensive session with a pastoral caregiver who had decades of experience as an inner-healing and deliverance minister. Overwhelmed by grief, I had a great need for understanding, affirmation, and encouragement. I recounted all the extreme sources of pain in my life. I wanted to know that what I was experiencing was normal Christianity, as opposed to being rejected or even punished by God.

At that time, my family was grieving the loss of five immediate family members who died one after another. In addition, a tornado swept through our town in Moore, Oklahoma and devastated it on the very day I buried my younger sister. My oldest daughter, who had been diagnosed with Rheumatoid Arthritis and had a baby out of wedlock, had just entered prison. My precious wife was struggling with a major health problem, a skin disorder brought on by stress. I personally suffered through the betrayal of two close friends who had falsely accused me of wrongdoing. I intensely grieved the loss of both my parents and faced bankruptcy even as I served the Lord in ministry. I also faced my own health problems. A few years earlier, I had to have emergency surgery to remove my gallbladder, and it was catching up—I experienced weight gain for the first time in my life! I was overwhelmed and felt depressed. The Christian life seemed much harder than I had imagined.

However, I came away from the day-long intensive counseling session with a more assured perspective: "many are the afflictions of the righteous, but the Lord delivers them from them all."[2]

God was **not angry** with me. I was not cursed, nor was I disqualified from Christian ministry as some had suggested. However, I felt very weak. I came away with an understanding that the only way the Lord might obtain my heart fully was to allow difficulties to purge me. I could choose to learn from the crucible of suffering or not. It was a call to embrace the dark night of the soul, as St. John of the Cross so eloquently foretold of the deeper Christian life. I had been called to rely on Jesus in a much deeper faith and to no longer depend on signs from heaven, such as a Holy Spirit witness. My pastoral caregiver helped me see that I was on a path, a journey to embrace an eternal perspective of what the mercy of God wanted to perfect in my life, so I might be made mature.

After the intensive session, I embraced the following life-changing and challenging biblical truths:

"The sufferings of this life are not to be compared to the glory that is to be revealed,"[3] and "the trials, the temptations and the sufferings of this life through godly endurance produce life-giving ripe fruit to those we will serve."[4]

These truths brought focus and gave me hope.

The Father had called me to wait patiently (with endurance) in suffering for the fruit in my life to be ripened. He did this so that I might be better equipped to serve with deep compassion those who also suffer.

I have repeatedly endeavored to know Jesus and to hear His voice. Many have cried out to *know* the Lord Jesus Christ. Crying out to *know* Jesus as Paul did, is to be intimately acquainted with Christ's rejection by men and to know a little about His death and resurrection as Paul did.

"But what things were gain to me, these I have counted loss for Christ. Yet indeed I also count all things loss for the excellence of the knowledge of Christ Jesus my Lord, for whom I have suffered the loss of all things, and count them as rubbish, that I may gain Christ and be found in Him, not having my own righteousness, which is from the law, but that which is through faith in Christ, the righteousness which is from God by faith; that I may **know Him** and the power of His resurrection, and the fellowship of His sufferings, being conformed to His death, if, by any means, I may attain to the resurrection from the dead.[5]

I needed this perspective for hope to rise and healing to be restored. I am so grateful for the solid truth given to me by my pastoral caregiver that day: "Blessed are those who endure various trials and tribulations in this life, for once they have endured and patiently waited on the Lord they will receive a crown of eternal life, promised to those who sincerely love the Lord Jesus Christ."[6]

Yet, how was I to endure that weight of sorrow or the great sorrow to come? These scriptural truths seemed more like a fairy tale and more than I was able to follow and obey.

By Jesus' Extreme Mercy and Favor, I Endured!

There is only one way for the healing balm of myrrh to flow; the tree of myrrh must be bruised for the tears of the balm to flow. The only way I could be a healthy offering of life, a gift to others, and a healing balm, was to endure bruising alongside Jesus Christ in my *little crosses*, in my *little life*.

In this sin-filled world, there is the Way, which is how the believer is matured into the likeness of Christ. This involves diligent surrender to God while simultaneously dying to our will. In this way, one lives to Him in the midst of pain. Living to His will means a *patient endurance* and an *eternal perspective* of suffering. The Scriptures refer to these as "momentary, light afflictions." An eternal perspective empowers the believer in Jesus. We must live with our eyes on eternity and a mindset that this life is truly but a vapor.[7]

We are called to live with this attitude—to set our mind on things above where Christ the Lord is seated as Creator, King, and Lord over us all.[8] Jesus has taught me to receive His gold, tried in fire, the gold of suffering that I may be clothed in righteousness.[9]

We can endure to the end. For once we have been tested and have resisted the Devourer, Jesus promises to strengthen, confirm, and establish us in righteousness for His glory and for our everlasting peace.[10]

Although there are seasons in life where you will certainly feel alone in the purifying of your faith, He is a faithful and loving God who will never leave nor forsake you.[11] All difficulties (and even chastening) does not seem pleasing, but our Lord is after the peaceable fruit of righteousness in our lives and a faith in Him that has been tested and is worth more than the purest of gold.[12]

No one has ever loved me more than my Savior, and no one will ever love you more than your Savior: the Creator of the Universe, the Lord Jesus Christ. My meditation on His cross, His passion, His grief, gives me life in my suffering and in my grief. The time I spend in meditation on the Creator God who died for my sins has always been fruitful. Meditation, quality time soaking in His loving passion on the cross, and release of my sin and darkness into His wounds, renews my life during my suffering and grief. Meditation on the passion of Christ gives life to those who remember a Savior who is acquainted with sorrow, grief, and great suffering.[13]

The perspective I gained through the help of my pastoral caregiver and through meditation on the suffering Christ has been great help in dealing with troubles that have come into my life. Many have asked how I was able to survive the pain of my childhood sexual abuse, bullying, the rapes and the beating I experienced as a teenager, and the grief of losing my parents and my two siblings. Truly, this kind of overwhelming grief is endured through knowing Christ on His cross. This is power; this is grace. It is the same message which prepares me for even greater challenges. It is how I process my *current grief* and the present pain of the ultimate challenge and loss: the death of my daughter, Charity Hope, who passed away in April of 2012.

Charity went into the hospital the very day I took a national stand against Alan Chambers and the Exodus board, warning the leaders of their segue to "gay Christianity" on April 20, 2012. I resigned my role as Chairman of the Ministry Council, removed First Stone Ministries as an Exodus member, and warned the Exodus leadership. I experienced so much pain from being mocked by several Exodus leaders, who prided themselves the most tolerant and loving people. They labeled me hateful, a man of divisiveness in exposing the heresy. The night of April 20, Charity entered the hospital with an unexplained mass growing rapidly in her brain. She coded the next morning and was gone. My precious daughter left this world! She was on life support for two more days, but the doctors told us she was gone; the decision was made to turn off the machines on April 24 at 12:30 AM. I felt as though my heart had been ripped out of my chest.

Yet, I know Him who knows my name and calls me into resurrection and gives me hope. I find Him in the suffering. I wait for Him in worship when I do not feel like worshipping. I wait for Him that I may have intimacy with Him now, and ultimately, that I may know Him in His resurrection. I embrace the character of the extravagant mercy of God who calls me into His likeness. He is the man of sorrows, who for the joy set before Him, endured all my evil at the cross.[14]

He is the *One* who joyfully embraced the suffering to have *you* as a prize. What amazing love!

Now, in this journey of life with its pain and sorrow as well as great joys, rather than yield to fleshly and addictive patterns when I am faced with suffering, I find my joy in Jesus through worship, meditating on His powerful, extravagant forgiveness, and through meditation on His words in the Gospels.

Ps. 1:2 "But his delight is in the law of the LORD, *and in His law he meditates day and night."*

Rather than yield to old ways, I seek out accountability and community in the body of Christ. This is a must on days that are dry and hard. In His community of believers, He pours His life into me in times of suffering and confession. The words from an intimate worship song by my friend, Dennis Jernigan, minister to me:

"The tree of myrrh is full of tears that only come falling when bruised, but the fragrant life that wounding brings is born on the wings of good news, like myrrh when hardened must be crushed before the fragrance can rise, my blinded heart must be made dust, so Father open my eyes. . ."

I am confident that He, who began this work in me, will complete it! (See Phil. 1:6).

To realize freedom, one must embrace a new lifestyle of suffering, dying to self, and yielding our life to Christ and others in the community of true believers. God gives His grace to the humble but resists the proud (James 4:6). We did not start this journey in our own strength, and we cannot finish it in our own strength. It truly is Jesus who started this work and He will complete it, *IF* we will merely yield to Him fully every day.

> To realize freedom, one must embrace a new lifestyle of suffering, dying to self, and yielding our life to Christ and others in the community of true believers. God gives His grace to the humble but resists the proud (James 4:6). We did not start this journey in our own strength, and we cannot finish it in our own strength.

Endnotes:
1. Matt. 10:21-23, Matt. 24:12-14, 1 Cor. 10:12-14, James 1:12, Rev. 2:7, 11, 17, 26, 3:5, 12, 21, 21:7
2. Psalm 34:18-19
3. Rom. 8:18
4. James 1:2-3, 1 Peter 1:6-8

5. Phil. 3:7-11
6. James 1:12
7. James 4:14
8. Col. 3:1-2
9. Rev. 3:18-20
10. 1 Peter 5:10-11
11. Heb. 13:5-6
12. Isa. 53:5, Heb. 12:9-11, 1 Peter 1:6-8
13. Isa. 53:4-6
14. Heb. 12:1-3

4

THE BURDEN OF THOSE WHO DO NOT FINISH THE RACE

"Never, never, never give up!" —*Winston Churchill*

"When it is a question of God's Almighty Holy Spirit, never say, 'I can't.'"
—*Oswald Chambers*

"I can do all things through Christ who strengthens me." —*Phil. 4:13*

I AM BURDENED FOR THOSE who return to homosexuality. I am sincerely broken over the many who have embraced false teachings—from the hyper-perverse-grace heresy to spirit guides who lure people back to the lie of homosexuality and "gay Christianity." I long for everyone I know to love God. Oh, for everyone to know His truth and experience His amazing grace that changed my life back in 1983. He continues to change my life to this day! However, I also have a greater burden for His church to be holy with ready answers to the questions raised by scoffers and those who proclaim "gay Christianity." Why do some start on a path of repentance only to return to their former sinful lifestyles? We need some answers. Although the reasons can be as complicated and diverse as people are, there are some conclusions I have reached after thirty years of ministry that are consistent.

Different Goals—Different Types of Seekers of Christ

Those of us who leave homosexuality and stay repentant share a vision and a goal that differs from those who embrace a "gay Christian" identity, which allows for the practice of homosexuality. Our fundamental belief—the foundation that drives lasting change—is not the same as those who relapse. Those who are consistent in their repentance embrace a process. They are overcomers. The overcomer never stops pressing in with eager desire for continued sanctification. This new way of living fosters a mature understanding of sanctification. This process requires a lifelong conformity to live like Christ. Our heart must long for a spiritual intimacy in a love relationship with God based upon belief in God's Word. We are, in effect, in love with Jesus Christ as our God. We have no other gods. We have faith in the Word of God even as we struggle. We are committed unto death to embrace a lifetime process to be conformed to His image. This process comes from a love relationship with God and a truly biblical worldview. As we understand and embrace grace (the power of God) in weakness and temptation, we know that homosexuality is not compatible with our faith in God. The result? A victor mentality that fuels the ability to live in repentance, we live a life of being strengthened even in weakness. (2 Cor. 12:710). True seekers in Christ find their identity in Him completely. Sincerely devoted people who leave homosexuality and same-sex lust behind do not look to psychology, higher learning, or gay advocates for the label of "gay" or "ex-gays", or a "sexual orientation." They look to Jesus Christ and His Word for their identity as male and female. The devoted believer is not deceived into embracing an identity of orientation or the desires of the fallen nature. Unfortunately, we have many today who communicate that same-sex attraction is a legitimate human condition; this has given rise to the "gay Christian" movement.

Those who embrace this false ideology tend to return to a life of sin. They become mockers. Time and again, those who label themselves "beyond ex-gay," "post-gay," "post-ex-gay" or "gay Christians," initially communicate a desire to change. Exasperated, they cry out, "CHANGE ME! Oh God, I want to be CHANGED!" Many sincerely look at their desires and truly wish to be fixed or changed. They believe the change of their desires must be met on their terms. They will come to a local ministry, to a church, or to God Himself, and demand a change of their attractions. They mock our ministries as "pray away the gay" organizations. Yet, ironically, this is exactly what they expect and demand, "pray away the gay" or ministry to gays is not real. Their demand is actually towards God. When the process includes more—more time, more seeking, more confession, more pressing into Jesus—they begin to consider other options. Not keeping their eyes totally fixed on Jesus Christ, they become fixated on the problem, their attractions, and their own unfettered lusts. They don't realize that life is but a vapor, and it make take the rest of their life to be made whole.

Unfortunately, they ultimately give up. Their belief for any change is for merely a season. It does not persevere. Whenever I have the opportunity to question these people and receive honest answers, I find they never have truly repented in their inner thought world. They constantly struggled with immoral thoughts and activities. There are many today in the church who have allowed psychology and sinful desires to engender the false ideas in their minds, which the corrupt fallen nature is beyond the transforming power of God. They call themselves "gay Christians." Sadly, the heresy spreads to family and friends who are affected by a loved one's struggle with same-sex attractions and who, themselves, become advocates of these distorted broken identities. It is heartbreaking to watch family members become worn down by gay theology, and

> What is worse, when embracing "orientation" comes from influential theologians keeping people in bondage to gay and unnatural desires with no real hope of transformative grace.

also lose their faith as they become sources of empowerment to these distortions. What is worse, when embracing "orientation" comes from influential theologians keeping people in bondage to gay and unnatural desires with no real hope of transformative grace. Those who return to homosexuality actually proclaim, "Jesus Christ alone is not enough!" They want to be delivered from the sufferings of doing battle with temptation with same-sex attractions and lust. In the end, they support the false claim that homosexuality must be compatible with Christianity.

But this begs a question: where did we get the idea we should be delivered from suffering? Christ never promised that we would not suffer in the flesh. In fact, He promised us that we would suffer and that we need to deny ourselves. Unfortunately, this resonates as victimization. In the face of suffering, some rebel against the biblical worldview and celebrate and embrace a gay identity. Many who are mockers of our ministries become completely intolerant of those who desire, by faith in God's Word, to leave homosexuality fully. Ironically, the very people who scream for tolerance are extremely intolerant of those who turn away from homosexual behavior and live by faith, not claiming any label.

The Problem with Suffering

Historically, there have always been a variety of motivations to seek Christ. The maturing Christian who wants to leave homosexuality behind understands that being a disciple of Jesus Christ entails suffering in the flesh and resisting internal desires. The problem with suffering is it becomes old after a time. The majority of the people I know who have returned to homosexuality did not give up selfish indulgence. Pornography use was never fully eliminated. With that, of course, masturbation is practiced. This continues to encourage fantasies and a demonic feeding of sexual perversion into the soul. In this, they wonder why they cannot stop their

> The modern church has forsaken true repentance with contrition which produces rejuvenated souls—people being truly born again. (2 Cor. 13:5)

lust or why their same-sex attractions are continued over time. Their idea of holiness (separated to God), is a much lower standard than is taught in the Scriptures. Instead, they lean on the teachings of secular psychology, which anoints them with the false teaching of homosexual "orientation." They also mix-in the ridiculous once-prayed-always-saved theology. The modern church has forsaken true repentance with contrition which produces rejuvenated souls—people being truly born again. (2 Cor. 13:5)

The problem with suffering in the flesh and contrition is that there is no remedy in this life. You either embrace the denying of self—dying to self and suffering in the flesh—or you think of yourself more highly than the words of our Lord Jesus Christ in His Gospel. Jesus' Gospel, the Good News, is redemption for those who truly surrender to Him by faith in what He has done for us on Calvary's cross. This sincere faith in His Gospel leads to repentance. When one embraces repentance, suffering aligns the soul for a full surrender to Jesus. No doubt, some will hold fast to the end, persevering in obedience to Christ without full relief of same-sex attraction, but it will no longer be a burning, uncontrollable lust. Same-sex attraction does not control them because Jesus has become their Lord. He is more desirable than their flesh or worldly desires. The

> The reality of suffering is that you cannot escape it in this life. You must accept it to become a mature man or woman of God.

reality of suffering is that you cannot escape it in this life. You must accept it to become a mature man or woman of God. "These things I have spoken to you, that in Me you may have peace. In the world, you will have tribulation (suffering), but be of good cheer, I have overcome the world." (John 16:33)

Gays and the Companion of Fools

Another reason that many fall back into sin is that they continue to keep in close association with those who practice homosexuality. If only those who struggle with same-sex attraction would take seriously the warnings in Scripture about sitting in the presence of foolish mockers. The warning is clear: if you are a companion of a fool, you will become a fool. If you sit with scoffers, their ways will penetrate your heart. Evil communication truly corrupts the soul.[1] When you look at the fall of Exodus International and other leaders who have embraced a gay identity and homosexuality, you see that these biblical warnings were not heeded. As a matter of fact, living by these warnings is often mocked as legalism. This was true of the fallen Exodus International leadership. The implosion of Exodus began by listening to so-called relevant messages rather than sound doctrine. This messaging easily transitions into the "emergent" message or the "nice gospel," where the messaging calls for believers to embrace worldliness. Many who start out as well-meaning, over time end up maligning biblical truths, specifically prophetic truths that extol freedom. These cool and relevant leaders will mock warnings, calling prophetic warnings too hard. They think themselves wiser than the old, tested ways. John the Baptist and most of the prophets of the Bible would not be allowed to enter this modern, sin-tolerating church.

There are leaders today who call the prophet voice of warning, "Jerks!" They teach their people to ignore these warnings because they are all under grace where there is no need to listen to warnings. Many churches today push out prophetic voices, and these people are leaving organized church. These cool Christian leaders and their followers are people today would say how unkind it was of God to turn Lot's wife into a pillar of salt for merely looking back to Sodom.

The Biblically Illiterate Church?

It is heartbreaking to watch those who return to a proud gay identity either as a celibate or as a practicing homosexual. Truly, both lifestyles are based on poor theology about redemption and the transformational grace promised to us in the Gospel of Jesus Christ. If you listen to "gay Christians" explain their dilemma, you find it based on self, and victimization by world systems and the mean church. It is true that the church in many places has been very unkind and unloving to the same-sex attracted struggler and to the practicing homosexual. Yet, the church that believes itself kinder than God, however, it is actually quite unloving to accept distorted identities. I will go into this subject more in the chapter, "Shall the Church Show Real Compassion?" Those who call themselves celibate "gay Christians" are usually not called to celibacy, but they are abstainers. I applaud the abstainer! This is commendable! However, celibacy is a call from God; it should not be based upon having same-sex attractions. Thank God, the abstainer knows that homosexual behavior is sinful and forbidden! Still, the sad truth for many of these abstainers is that they have embraced a false identity as a struggling sexual human being. God has much more for them, usually a call to marriage if, in fact, they have a strong sex drive. Unfortunately, these "gay Christian" abstainers refuse to denounce the label and the practice of being gay. They embrace those who actively participate in homosexual behavior. Both groups, the celibate "gay Christian" and the practicing homosexual who still claim a Christian identity, show a profound depth of biblical illiteracy. "Therefore, if anyone is in Christ, he *is* a new creation; old things have passed away; behold, all things have become new." (2 Cor. 5:17).

The more egregious situation is the pack of people mixed together who are embraced by the church as mere suffering, same-sex attracted souls, rather than people who truly need maturity in sanctification. They have minimized grace to merely mean forgiven or receiving unmerited favor. They make believing in Jesus a mental assent to the historical facts rather than embracing a life-changing power. Instead of pressing on towards the goal of being in Jesus and becoming more like Him, they call for the church to accept same-sex attracted or "gay Christian" as their identities.

The grace of God teaches and empowers the soul to deny ungodliness in word, thought, and deed. The Spirit of grace, the very presence of Jesus in us as the Holy Spirit, brings transformation to the yielded soul. Never accept less! These people believe they are authentic when they embrace the flesh and their desires. They are told authenticity is good and to accept the inner world of same-sex attraction. Just accept yourself and you'll have peace. They are told these distortions repeatedly. The biblically illiterate church does not teach spiritual warfare and taking *every* thought captive to the obedience of Jesus Christ as Lord. This was one of the very first principles of freedom I was taught by my first pastor, John Ward (2 Cor. 10:3-5). I have memorized and meditated on this passage since the first month I was saved in 1983. However, we must be doers of this passage to find lasting freedom. The realignment of our thinking is imperative. We are not to be conformed to this world, but be transformed by the renewing of our minds, especially our internal world of sensuality. (Rom. 12:1-2).

Let's look at the biblical foundations for freedom, which enable us to separate ourselves from the world's values and our own appetites.

Laying Foundations for Freedom

How do we receive anything from God? How are we saved, delivered or freed? It is by grace through faith! The secular human mind struggles to grasp the meaning of faith, which is "the substance of

> Their internal world of thinking is not transformed for the "gay Christian."

things hoped for, the evidence of things not seen." (Heb. 11:1) Still, it is impossible to please God without a life of faith, which comes by hearing, listening to, and believing the Word of God. We must obey His Word and hear God in prayer. We cannot see faith! The ex-gay, or the former homosexual, lives by this consistent reality of faith. The beyond ex-gay, post ex-gay or the ex-ex-gay, lives in and for his or her appetites, desires and attractions. It is a startling difference. Jesus, reflecting on His second coming, asks, "Will I find faith on Earth?" (Luke 18:8).

Living by faith transforms our lives. Beyond ex-gay, ex-ex-gay, post ex-gay, and "gay Christians" do not want to believe in a faith with suffering. Their internal world of thinking is not transformed for the "gay Christian." As they journey, they embrace a false peace in a broken identity. Their internal world of thinking is not marked by integrity, nor by the fear of God. The "gay Christian" has simply resolved themselves that this is as good as it gets and surrenders to the lies of this age, listening to the wrong voices.

The Apostle Peter warned us that scoffers and mockers would come on the scene with louder and louder voices in the last days. Ruled by their own fleshly desires and seduced by demonic powers, Peter warned that the scoffers and mockers would come against those who desire to live godly lives. "Where is the promise of Jesus' deliverance and freedom?" they will mock. "*He* made us this way!" "Where is the promise of His coming?" they will say, "It has always been this way! You cannot change!"

(2 Peter 3:34, 1 Tim. 4:12, 2 Tim. 3:17, 2 Tim. 4:14, Matt. 5:11-12, Mark 13:9-13, Matt. 24:9-13).

Beloved, without condemnation, our hearts need to be moved with pity and intercession for these who are deceived and have fallen way. It is by grace we are saved. Truly, grace allows us to see. In grace, we must offer hope and mercy to those who continue to be burdened with a homosexual existence or a gay identity. But sincere love requires that we not compromise the truth by encouraging people to embrace a broken identity. Paul reminded us in Romans 9 of the kind of love in which we should partake: a profound love (wherein we at least weep with great mourning) and a greater love willing to die and even be accursed from Christ so they may be saved. I expound upon these ideas more fully in the chapters ahead, which deal with how Christ's redemptive power helps us to realize true and complete freedom.

Endnotes:
1. Ps. 1, Job 21:16, Ps. 1, Ps. 26:4, Prov. 1:10, Prov. 4:14-15, 1 Cor. 15:33

5

REAL HOPE—HOW FREEDOM IS REALIZED

"When His disciples heard it, they were greatly astonished, saying,
'Who then can be saved?'
But Jesus looked at them and said to them,
'With men this is impossible, but with God all things are possible.'"
—Matt. 19:25-26

IN THE LAST CHAPTER, WE looked at the process of those who actually experience freedom and examined some reasons why people find it hard to finish the race. It is a process! For many, this process of walking out freedom will be a battle for the rest of their lives. This is especially true for those who have lived gay-identified and embraced homosexual behavior for several years. For those who have simply battled same-sex attraction as a young person and have yielded their lives to Christ and did not embrace homosexual behavior, their battle will be significantly less challenging, *if* they continue in the faith, yielding to the warnings prescribed in Scripture and receive the necessary help found in the previous chapter, An Overview of Homosexuality. In that chapter and in this one, I reveal truths, long-tested over many years of ministry, that demonstrate how hope and freedom become real and lasting.

Living by Faith

"Enter by the narrow gate; for wide is the gate and broad is the way that leads to destruction, and there are many who go in by it. Because narrow is the gate and difficult is the way which leads to life, and there are few who find it" (Matt. 7:13-14). According to Jesus, the way is narrow, not broad, as has been taught in many of our modern churches. Jesus tells us the way is very narrow and few find it. Yet, have you ever been to a funeral of a practicing sinner whose life was marked with worldly living? It seems, in the modern church, everyone goes to heaven. They teach that this can happen by merely praying a prayer. So, what are the percentages? Does the Scripture reveal anything? As a matter of fact, it does.

When Jesus relates the parable of the sower in Mark 4, He tells us the sober truth that only a small percentage of those who hear the Word of God will experience lasting transformation in their hearts. They will not conform to His image of self-denial. Gay "theology" completely ignores this foundational teaching. When Jesus explained Mark 4:1-20, He was telling us that it was extremely important to understand this parable in order to understand all the other parables. He warns us to understand that the "birds of the air" (symbolizing Satan), come to steal truth from the heart, even as it is delivered. This is the real warning of spiritual warfare that we as believers must heed. According to this parable, only one quarter hear and respond righteously and bear good fruit. In light of that truth, as expressed by Christ, I am grateful that we have the statistics showing success revealed by The FSM Effectiveness Survey. The reality is that 73 percent of those who diligently seek help through our ministry find lasting freedom. This shatters Alan Chambers' supposition that 99.9 percent don't change. Incidentally, here is one amazing statistic related to Jesus' earthly ministry: He only had one of His twelve apostles betray Him and fall away—Judas Iscariot. That is an even more amazing statistic: a 92 percent success rate!

The Word of God

The foundation for freedom can never go any further than where the bedrock of faith begins. The "gay Christian" movement and those who discredit ministries such as First Stone or the Restored Hope Network, can only do so by discrediting biblical truth and skewing Scripture to their own desires. What does the Bible say is the greatest enemy of the Christian life? **Unbelief.** Hebrews 3:7-19 tells us that unbelief means we do not believe what God has clearly written within the pages of the Bible. Unable to believe the Scriptures from the heart, scoffers must explain away the verses that condemn homosexual behavior. This unbelief is based upon the oldest lie in the Bible: a questioning of God and His character. Just like Satan in the Garden of Eden, scoffers with their doubts ask, "Has God really said?" (Gen. 3:1). Romans 1 confirms, "For they exchanged the truth of God for a lie." (vs.25). According to James 1:21-22 and 1 Peter 1:22-25, we must receive the truth of God's Word implanted into our hearts for our salvation.

Tragically, desires and lust in a spirit of unbelief trump the truth of God's Word for many. They simply will not endure to the end, and why should they when so many people tell them it is okay to be a "gay Christian?" Beloved, by the end of this decade, you will be surprised by some of the most influential leaders that are going to capitulate! Will you believe the Word of God or embrace the favor of men?

The Beginning of Wisdom

Wisdom from God is certainly the foundation of freedom to live a godly life. What is the beginning of walking in God's wisdom? Where do we discover the source of wisdom from God? How do we learn? Rest assured that when the Scriptures repeat something it is because it is very important. How important is a subject if it is repeated over and over, dozens of times? I would say extremely important!

The beginning of wisdom is found in the understanding that God is holy and should be revered in an intimate relationship. (Prov. 9:10). Those who live in rebellion need to fear His divine wrath. Truly, God is awesome, and we should live in awe of Him. I repeat; when the Bible speaks to a topic a few times, we should take it very seriously. The following are just some of the verses on this vital subject of wisdom: Psalms 19:9; 25:14; 111:10; Proverbs 1:7; 8:13; 9:10; 14:26-27; 15:33; 16:6; 19:23; 22:4. Clearly, we see in all these passages of Scripture that there is great wisdom in knowing the fear of God.

Unfortunately, today's church sends conflicting messages. One message offers a Jesus who will make you happy and blessed—a better you. The other message tells us we should be grateful that a holy God frees us from destruction. This message describes a God who loved us enough to die for our sins even though we deserve hell. In a "gay Christian" environment, hell is not preached accurately (Rev. 21:7-8), if at all. The beginning of wisdom may be touched on to teach how Christ died to deliver us from hell. However the necessity of suffering in our flesh in this life to be free from inordinate desires such as being driven with same-sex lust would not be mentioned.

The teaching of hell is mostly mocked in "gay Christian" environments. It certainly is not appreciated in many circles of ministry in the church. Yet Christ mentioned hell more than heaven in His own teachings. These truths are not taught or believed by gay-affirming "Christians" who endorse homosexual behavior. The sincere love of God compels us to deliver souls from eternal destruction (James 5:20). This is such an important subject and is truly the spiritual DNA of my soul that keeps me holy and sober. I will never stop teaching and preaching this as a core principle for freedom. It is imperative for the maturing Christian.

Therefore, I have devoted the chapter, Coram Deo—Experience Freedom in His Presence, to emphasize the importance of this subject.

A.B.S.

A core strength for a human being is a strong rectus abdominis muscle, also known as the abdominals or abs. Our spiritual body must also have strong core strength! We need spiritual ABS as a foundation for freedom. Just as our physical abs must be worked out to be strong for freedom to be fully realized, our spiritual muscles must be worked out to enjoy a new life. I have ministered in the area of freedom from sexual sin and brokenness for over thirty years. I know of no one who walks in real, consistent freedom from any kind of sin without these strong ABS:

A—Accountability. Accountability is a core strength, essential to lasting and consistent freedom. Accountability is found as we live in community with other believers and enjoy life together. This provides the natural process to confess our sins to each other and receive healing prayer. If we confess and forsake our sin, we find great mercy. Godly accountability is more than a dreaded confession session; it is life in a community where accountability becomes natural in a safe environment of holy, healthy relating. Healthy accountability becomes a haven of comfort and safety and not of condemnation. (James 5:16 and Prov. 28:13). This is true accountability, and it must be demonstrated by leaders before their disciples.

B—Boundaries. We all need boundaries set in place to separate us from temptation. We must appropriately distance ourselves from people, places, things, and activities that draw us into sin. Anything that draws our hearts away into temptation must have boundaries. If we view boundaries as restrictions rather than protections, we already enter a state of defeat. When a boundary is considered a restriction, we enter into immature and unwise thinking. A wise person understands one's own areas of weakness. Weakness does not reflect a defect of character.

It merely reveals a place of vulnerability. If we truly want freedom, we must view boundaries as protection, as safety, and embrace them as comforting. We all need boundaries on our computers and from all bad influences in order to walk in integrity. No one is immune in this day. We must protect ourself and our loved ones. Truly, as a foundation for freedom, a person must establish boundaries in every area of life that is a place of potential temptation.

S—Spiritually-Devoted Life, Practicing Spiritual Warfare. We must practice spiritual warfare as a core principle of freedom, for we wrestle not against flesh and blood but are in a spiritual battle. We truly wrestle against Satan and his hordes of demonic hosts. Ephesians chapter 6, verse 12 is a passage that must be believed. One should review this verse in several translations. Here is a look at it in *The Living Bible*, which is a paraphrased version:

> *For we are not fighting against people made of flesh and blood, but against persons without bodies—the evil rulers of the unseen world, those mighty satanic beings and great evil princes of darkness who rule this world; and against huge numbers of wicked spirits in the spirit world.*

This passage gives the perspective of a fight against unseen forces. What would you do to fight against a band of invisible enemies coming to kill and destroy your family? That is precisely what is taking place. Unfortunately, many people in the church do not believe this passage, nor do they actually resist the devil in their lives. If you knew that there were a host of men coming to kill your family, wouldn't you at least dial 911 and put up a fight? We must fight for the domain of our souls. This battle is real, against actual invisible forces. No one walks in real freedom without resisting these enemies!

A spiritually-devoted life must include full practice and participation in Christian disciplines to renew the mind, will, and emotions. If we are spiritually devoted, we will read God's Word and meditate on His truths daily, pray and fast, journal, maintain consistent fellowship with believers, and daily worship the Creator of the Universe—Jesus Christ. Where there is true intimacy, it is easy to worship Him daily in the majesty of all we see around us in the creation. He is not a far-off God to those who have a sincere, devoted spiritual life. Jesus Christ is an intimate friend, the lover of our soul. If you have not experienced this, then oh, beloved, there is so much more for you! Freedom can be realized! When we have this type of relationship, we are always ready to tell others of our faith as witnesses of Christ's great love to save sinners. This also increases the boundaries of the heart of the believer to expect more. As we bear witness to what Christ has done for us, our faith increases! It is a means of grace. As believers, we also need to practice the sacramental institutions of communion and baptism. If you have never been baptized as an adult, you should consider doing so with a pastoral care-giver. Once you have done so, it is imperative for the believer to practice a lifestyle of communion in fellowship with the Lord Jesus Christ in His meal. You renew your covenant love with Him at each holy communion.

Those who fail, fall back, and embrace a gay identity, do not have this kind of spiritual devotion. They do not have ABS. If you live openly, honestly, and transparently, you will find freedom. If you cover up and live in darkness, unbelief and lies will find a lodging place in your soul, which becomes a nest for the enemy. Secretiveness empowers sin and corrupts the soul. Living in the light dispels darkness and keeps the darkness dispelled. His light gives life to the soul, for God is light, and in Him there is no darkness. (1 John 1:5).

True transparency brings all hidden weakness into the light with safe accountability. This is why confession is considered a sacrament by many in the church, especially Catholics. Confession is a means of grace for holiness for all believers. James 5:16 says, *"Confess your trespasses to one another, and pray for one another, that you may be healed. The effective, fervent prayer of a righteous man avails much."* This shows us the pattern of confession to one another and the much needed power of prayer. This brings healing and is never more evident than in a true disciple of Jesus Christ and a prayer warrior. The warrior is going to practice spiritual warfare and pray! One of the main areas of weakness in those who fall back is that they did not practice spiritual warfare consistently. Second Corinthians 10:3-5 was not a passage they memorized nor put into practice. They may not have understood it, or perhaps they were lazy in their thought life. Either way, demonic activity always comes to condemn. Condemnation is a joy killer. There is nothing joyful about being filled with shame and condemnation. In fact, these things only bring discouragement. This is a key tactic of demonic spirits and the reason we must have a diligent, spiritually-devoted life where we practice spiritual warfare.

Mentorship

Those who overcome homosexuality and find lasting freedom develop right relationships with the same sex. One of the greatest needs for those who find freedom is to become secure in their own gender. This can often begin in parental relationships. Men and women who repair broken relationships with parents to the best of their ability receive a blessing on their lives (Mal. 4:6, Ex. 20:12). Men and women who develop healthy relationships within the church—men with men and women with women—embrace the restoration of biblical gender identity and find freedom. This can be a difficult process, but is necessary for freedom. I have never known anyone who walks in true freedom who does not comply with this much-needed healing component of healthy relating.

Complete Inner Healing

The Spirit of the LORD is upon me, because He has anointed me to preach the gospel to the poor; He has sent me to heal the brokenhearted, to proclaim liberty to the captives and recovery of sight to the blind, to set at liberty those who are oppressed; to proclaim the acceptable year of the LORD. (Luke 4:18-19)

Many times, when Christians hear, "inner healing" they judge it as secular or silly therapy. However, it was Jesus who said that He came to heal the brokenhearted. Beloved, this is inner healing. Unfortunately, many merely start the process of allowing the Lord to heal some of their histories of brokenness. Our Western mindset of drive-by-Christianity gives us the expectation that change will happen quickly. However, for many people, inner healing and transformation of the soul, the mind, the memories, the will, and the emotions can take years. This is why counseling and talk therapy is so helpful. Professional Christian counselors can help the same-sex attracted person unpack many unresolved issues. There are many capable pastoral care providers in the Restored Hope Network. Many underlying issues can be traumatic, cause gender confusion, and broken sexually-addictive behaviors. It requires humility. For some people, this can mean several years of contrite brokenness in counseling. There may be relapses, and some back-and-forth until a person starts a path of consistency. Then, freedom can be realized. Those who are open to the power of the Holy Spirit in His timing find this healing much quicker than most. This process brings us to the cross of Jesus Christ.

The Work of the Cross

"For the message of the cross is foolishness to those who are perishing, but to us who are being saved it is the POWER OF GOD." (1 Cor. 1:18)

When I think of this verse, I am always reminded of the Living Waters program developed by Andrew Comiskey. The DNA of Living Waters is to become centered in the life-giving power of Jesus' crucifixion for our redemption. First Corinthians 1:18 is not merely a beginning place of Christianity. The preaching of the cross is salvation for the surrendered soul. This is what Andrew Comiskey has masterfully given the church in his program, Living Waters. It helps souls navigate through all the broken root causes I mentioned in Overview of Homosexuality. His program brings them to the cross.

Crucifixion is a place of death. In His wisdom and sovereignty, the God of the universe chose the time of Roman crucifixion to send His Son to die a terrible death in our place and redeem mankind. God's wisdom, to choose a horrible death through great suffering, transcends human understanding. But it is a powerful reminder that He understands suffering. The power of God rests upon those who trust in God in their own suffering. Those who understand this foundational teaching will walk in freedom through the knowledge that God did not promise to deliver us from suffering, but He does promise to impart grace to us, to empower us, and to cause us to rise above the suffering of our temptations and broken histories. We must come to the cross daily and bring our pain and temptations. By faith, we must release our grief, our shame, and our sin into the body of Jesus at the cross. There, we must release all our hopes, dreams, desires, and attractions. Suffering is God's unexpected pathway to great joy if endured to the end. The cross is *life* to those who believe and put their faith in what Jesus Christ accomplished there. As we endure to the end, we deny ourselves and live for His glory.

Meditation of the Passion of Our Lord

The cross is what brings us into an intimate relationship with God. As we spend time in meditation on all the ways our Lord suffered, it is a sure pathway to align our soul to die to self. Jesus not only died a terrible death, but He left heaven to become man. He was born into human flesh. He was placed in a feeding trough for cows. He was born in a barn. The King of glory chose this entry to begin His redemption plan. Meditation on when He decided to come, His history, His words, and His life give us perspective. True meditation on the stations of the cross in the Gospels during lent is extremely helpful. There are many writings on the meditations of the sufferings of Christ. This is a means of grace in finding lasting freedom. We have never suffered, nor will we ever suffer, as much as Jesus did. Oh! How He still does in seeing the breadth of sin's ravages on the creation. These truths give us strength just as Paul's words encouraged the Philippians in chapter 1, verse 21 and chapter 2, verses 5-11. Only through the meditations of the passion of Jesus Christ and believing upon the finished work of the cross of Christ can we ever hope to really be free!

> Only through the meditations of the passion of Jesus Christ and believing upon the finished work of the cross of Christ can we ever hope to really be free!

Prayer Life

It was Leonard Ravenhill who said, "Let me spend an hour with a man in prayer and I will tell you about his true spiritual condition." Leonard Ravenhill is one of many men to whom I attribute my spiritual formation. His encouragement and exhortation to pray has forever changed my life. I do not advocate judging people based upon an hour of prayer, but a man's prayer life will determine his level of spiritual maturity. Ravenhill knew what he was talking about. Men and women who walk in consistent freedom are intent on knowing God in prayer. To experience God in prayer is a consistent and diligent discipline.

My experience with those who find lasting freedom is that they have passion and fire in their prayers. Jesus asked his disciples, "Could you not tarry with Me just one hour?" I believe the Lord asks that same question today of believers. "Can you not just spend one hour with Me?" One of several reasons people do not succeed and break free from sexual brokenness is that they do not have a diligent prayer life, which is needed to support victorious spiritual warfare. Prayer should include worship with a very grateful heart—for gratefulness is the will of God for the believer in Christ. (1 Thess. 5:18). Many use prayer to complain or present a laundry list of needs. These things can be a place to start in prayer, but the prayer life must mature far beyond a lists of wants. As mentioned before, our fight is not against flesh and blood. People become weary in the battle because of prayerlessness. But remember, the enemy we face is real and relentless. Therefore, our prayer life must be consistent. Do you enjoy prayer? Until you can answer an honest yes, you will not find the depth of freedom you need.

Conquering Unforgiveness and Shame

Never be unaware of the deliberate schemes of Satan. He always comes with offense. When we are angry and become offended, we provide an opportunity for Satan to cause us to be critical and defiled. (Eph. 4:26-27). He causes the heart to be divided with bitterness, so the very strongholds of sexual sin will storm back in like a flood. Satan then brings his condemnation and paralyzes the solider with shame to retreat into darkness (Matt. 6:12, Matt. 18, 2 Cor. 2:10-11, Rev. 12:10-11, Rom. 8:1). This is a real scheme of Satan and one many are not aware of because they hide in shame.

God's Love Is the Conclusion

The foundation for freedom and healing is to cultivate a life goal that longs for heaven. This is the longing of maturing believers: they long to hear the Father say, "Well done thy good and faithful servant. Enter into the joy of heaven." This is the essence of the spiritual life for those who realize freedom, longing for Jesus. Those who overcome will be clothed in white raiment, given authority to rule with God and live eternally. Those who identify themselves as beyond ex-gay, post ex-gay or ex-ex-gay, say change does not work because they have not thoroughly given their entire life process in commitment to the Lord to deny self and live to God only. They have a distorted perspective on what life is all about and just how short this earthly existence is in light of eternity. The truth is clear from the Bible: life is but a vapor, and we must live by faith in God, believing and trusting in Him. "Fight the good fight of faith, lay hold of eternal life, to which you were also called and have confessed the good confession." (1 Tim. 6:12, Col. 1:23). God gives His power, and His grace, to the humble. (James 4:4-10, 1 Peter 5:5-10). Yet many demand that God should do a work of freedom from their suffering and temptation, which He, in His wisdom, does not necessarily give. Those who have gone back into homosexuality, gave up too soon. After all, an entire life waiting on Jesus is still nothing more than a vapor in eternity. Those who return to their old ways, into a life of sin, will live with painful regret for all eternity.

God is love, and His ways are so much higher than ours. His plan for us is to love in such a way that we would be like the Apostle Paul in Romans 9:13, with great sorrow to be perfected in love and a deeper willingness to be accursed

> Those who have gone back into homosexuality, gave up too soon. After all, an entire life waiting on Jesus is still nothing more than a vapor in eternity. Those who return to their old ways, into a life of sin, will live with painful regret for all eternity.

from Christ, so others would have eternal life. This is godly and mature Christian living. The surrendered church continues to grow in this extravagant love. Unfortunately, this kind of love is not demonstrated in much power in the church at large, at least not yet. This is why so many are without hope. May the Lord grant us His power to represent this manifestation of His love so that we may give hope to those who are falling away and see many restored who had returned into a lifestyle of sin and worldliness. For no one who is controlled by the love of God wants a soul to have regret for all eternity.

6

CORAM DEO–EXPERIENCE FREEDOM IN HIS PRESENCE

"The LORD *takes pleasure in those who fear Him, in those who hope in His mercy." —Ps. 147:11*

Know and Understand—Coram Deo

CORAM DEO IS LATIN, TRANSLATED as a phrase, "in the presence of God" In historic church theology, Coram Deo communicates the truth of Christians living in the presence, under the authority, and to the honor and glory of God at all times.

Coram Deo is living in a cognizant state of being before the face of God. To live in the presence of God is to understand that whatever we do and wherever we do it, we are before the gaze of Almighty God. God is omnipresent. Therefore, there is no place that we can escape His penetrating gaze. *HE sees!* Coram Deo is to live with a conscience state of awareness of His sovereignty. We enjoy His terrible awesomeness and fear God when we encounter this relationship like a fountain of life as we read in Proverbs 14:27: *"The fear of the* LORD *is a fountain of life, to turn one away from the snares of death."*

Coram Deo also means to be overwhelmed by God's love, to be in awe of Him because He is so forgiving and merciful. Only those who are truly born of the Holy Spirit can understand this dual awesomeness! God is terrible, fearful, and full of awe! God is NOT tame, He is NOT safe, but He is oh so very good! Oh so holy, so merciful, and so loving. Without understanding the duality of holy severity and the incredible kindness of God, we cannot grow into true Christian maturity, nor will we realize the depths of freedom available to us in His presence.

Coram Deo living is wrapped-up in the *fear* of God, and the *fear* of God is *not* mere reverential trust. One merely need ask those who have truly received a glimpse of God or peer into the Holy Scriptures and read about those who have encountered God in His glory (Rev. 1:12-17). They fall in awe, in terrible fear—*trembling* before the Almighty! God has transformed my life through Coram Deo. I pray that you embrace Coram Deo yourself to experience that great freedom He has for those who love Him! Living in the full awareness and knowledge of **Coram Deo** ensures a victorious life that is free from sin bondage. You can see this in a study of the promises found in Scriptures in endnote 1 of this chapter.

Holy prophets are rarely embraced or accepted during their office in this life. Real prophets live in Coram Deo. It is why they communicate very stark, specific, and distinctly bold pronouncements against sin as they warn of the soul's destruction. Today, most of the church would not welcome such holy prophets of old, believing themselves smarter, more sophisticated, and more refined. Indeed, they are more refined—so refined most of the time as to passively empower sin to remain in the hearts of people. This is one reason why I believe so many continue to struggle with same-sex attraction. The church, and even many in the ranks of ex-gay ministry, feel they must have a message that is kinder, nicer and more compassionate than the leadership in the Bible. It is true that most people today cannot stomach hearing bold, passionate preaching, and rarely is there a message on the torments of hell.[1]

Truly, we have embraced a more effeminate, breathy, and timid gospel message with trendy messengers. This is a result of years of browbeating by the LGBTQ+ activist saying that the church is hateful. No doubt, the "church" in many places has been unkind and yes, even hateful. One example of true hate is the wickedness of the "God Hates Fags!"–Westboro Baptist gang. This gang is not Christian. They reject salvation and redemption for the repentant homosexual. We must not allow false accusations of hate to keep us from loving the world enough to declare and teach the unaltered, unedited, powerful truth of God's Word—especially to the sexual sinner.

> For freedom to really permeate same-sex attracted souls and anyone else held in bondage to any sin, the revelation of **Coram Deo**—knowing the fear of God—must be restored.

We need to be empowered by the Holy Spirit for revival. In church history, true heaven-breathed revival has always come as a result of much prayer—even years of prayer, along with constant and bold preaching of repentance. For freedom to really permeate same-sex attracted souls and anyone else held in bondage to any sin, the revelation of **Coram Deo**—knowing the fear of God—must be restored. This is precisely, the extremely important message for my own spiritual foundation for freedom. True spiritual formation for real freedom must have, "the beginning of wisdom."[2] There are far too many people who pervert the teaching of the fear of God to instead minimize His holiness and make a god in their own image. Unfortunately, they leave many in bondage to same-sex lust and many other forms of sin as they proclaim a cheap-grace message and mere reverential trust.

"It is good that you take hold of one thing (righteousness/compassion/ kindness) and also not let go of the other (wisdom/the fear of God/severity); for the one who fears and worships God [with awe-filled reverence] will come forth with both of them." (Ecc. 7:18. AMP Parenthetical added.)

CORAM DEO — God sees you, all the time. He knows everything you do, and one day you will give account to HIM when you die.

"For the Word of God is living and active, sharper than any two-edged sword, piercing to the division of soul and of spirit, of joints and of marrow, and discerning the thoughts and intentions of the heart. And no creature is hidden from His sight (God sees all), but all are naked and exposed to the eyes of Him to whom we must give account." (Jesus Christ—The Word of God—will be our judge). (Heb. 4:12 & 13 AMP)

"For we know Him who said, 'Vengeance is mine; I will repay.' And again, 'The Lord will judge His people.' It is a fearful thing to fall into the hands of the living God." (Heb. 10:30 & 31 AMP)

"Let us therefore, receiving a kingdom that is firm and stable and cannot be shaken, offer to God pleasing service and acceptable worship, with modesty and pious care and godly fear and in trembling awe; for our God [is indeed] a consuming fire." (Heb. 12:28 & 29 AMP)

MAY WE GROW IN CORAM DEO FOR JESUS' SAKE AND FOR GOD'S GLORY!

Endnotes:
1. Read the "Terrors of Hell" by William C. Nichols (http://www.firststone.org/articles/post/the-terrors-of-hell).

2. When the Bible teaches us something more than once, it is very important. When the Bible communicates a truth many times, it is extremely important to God. When a truth subject is communicated over and over, it is truly a matter of life and death. Over fifty verses noted here that are promises for you in the Bible concerning the fear of God. Here are some: Deut. 6:1-9, Ps. 19:9, 33:18, 34:7-11, 66:16, 85:9, 103:11-17, 111:10, 145:19, 147:11, Prov. 1:7, 1:29, 2:5, 8:13 9:10 10:27, 14:26-27, 15:16, 15:33, 16:6, 19:23, 22:4, 23:17, Ecc. 12:13, Isa. 11:1-3, Matt. 10:28, Luke 1:50, Luke 12:5, Luke 23:40, Acts 9:31, 10:35, 13:16 & 26, Col. 3:22, 1 Peter 2:17, Rev. 14:7, Rev. 19:5

7

SO-CALLED "GAY CHRISTIANITY" AND THE GOSPEL ACCORDING TO JESUS CHRIST

"For I am not ashamed of the gospel of Christ, for it is the (transformative) power of God to salvation for everyone who believes..."
—Rom. 1:16

The goal of our instruction, (our gospel) is love from a pure heart and a good conscience and a sincere faith. (see 1 Tim. 1:5)

"If anyone teaches a different doctrine and does not agree with the sound words of our Lord Jesus Christ, and to the doctrine and teaching which is in agreement with godliness, (personal integrity, upright behavior), he is conceited and woefully ignorant, understanding nothing..." —1 Tim. 6:3-4

THE GOSPEL ACCORDING TO JESUS Christ is the same message for a gay-identified person, an idolater, an adulterer, a fornicator, a pornographer, a liar, a thief, a gossip, a slanderer or a murderer. The message of good-news–redemption into a love relationship with God is the same for all sinners.[1] Many church leaders communicate a message

115

that is not biblical, but instead is deceptive and eternally dangerous. It is not a message of love when church leaders lead a person into a false hope. Unfortunately, this misleading message of "gay Christianity" is spread by perhaps well-meaning but biblically-illiterate leaders. They present a message based not on the truth of the Bible, but on a man-made theology mixed with secular psychology. Other leaders purposefully spread this false message, knowing its deceptive roots—a much graver offense. Still, others have consciously decided not to teach on homosexual sin at all so as not to offend those in attendance. But this is still in and of itself, deception. The words of Dietrich Bonhoeffer come to mind here. For those who are unfamiliar, Bonhoeffer was a Christian, a pastor, and a teacher who lived out his faith and proclaimed the Word of God even as the incredible evils of Nazism captured the hearts and minds of his home country, Germany.

"Silence in the face of evil is itself evil: God will not hold us guiltless. Not to speak is to speak. Not to act is to act." —Dietrich Bonhoeffer

Deception that leads people astray is not love; it is evil.[2] Deception that deliberately omits uncomfortable, soul-saving truth is not love; it is evil. I share this chapter with the same grief-filled compassion as expressed by the Apostle Paul to the Romans in Romans 9:1-3.[3] Here he wrote "with a great heavy heart and many tears." Paul reminded us that many will fall away from the faith in the last days.[4] This perversion of the true Gospel is an example of the message of ease, love of pleasure, and living unrepentantly with which many will go astray.[5] For more in-depth biblical study (over 150 verses), please see the references and endnotes which accompany this chapter. As you read, let God's Word be your guide. Reading God's Word as a companion with this chapter will promote *freedom realized* for you.

Good News or Bad?

The Gospel is Good News from Creator God, the Father in heaven, revealed to us through Jesus Christ, the Son of God. It is an amazing message of love given to fallen humanity.[6] By believing and abiding in Christ, the believer's relationship with Holy God is restored to the way it was before the fall. The Good News is that God the Father has made a way for all mankind to be restored to His original, divine intent of an intimate loving relationship that is greater than any we will experience in this fallen world. His desire is for you to be *forever* with Him.[7]

Many proclaim a message that totally contradicts the Gospel of Jesus Christ: you can be a practicing sexually-immoral person or a practicing homosexual and go to heaven. The Bible speaks directly to this with uncompromised clarity.[8] The truth expressed in Ephesians 5:5 is very clear: you can **know** with ***certainty*** that **no one** who practices sexual immorality will go to heaven. (See NASB). Interestingly, the Bible often follows these types of passages with the reminder that we should ***not be deceived*** by people who spout empty promises or words that contradict the truth.[9]

Jesus came to save us from and out of our sins, not leave us in them.[10] A person who struggles with sin differs from a person who embraces and freely practices sin. The Good News is that Jesus died for the sins of the world and rose victoriously over death, hell, and the devil. When Christ rose from the dead, He gave us the promise of the Holy Spirit of grace,[11] assuring us that the Holy Spirit would come and live in those truly born of God unto eternal life. The Holy Spirit of grace empowers true believers to live holy, repentant lives in a devout relationship with Jesus Christ as Lord. However, the Spirit does ***not*** live in people who are hostile towards God and disobedient, embracing and practicing sexual

> Jesus came to save us from and out of our sins, not leave us in them.

immorality.[12] The Bible tells us the Holy Spirit is given to those who obey God.[13] The Bible also tells us that **all** sexual immorality grieves God. Our holy heavenly Father is revealed in the person of the Holy Spirit, who will **never** abide with, or approve of, any immoral behavior.[14] God opposes the proud and gives His grace, the Spirit of Grace, to those who humble themselves and see their need for Christ.[15] **Anyone** who says otherwise is not teaching the whole Gospel of Jesus Christ[16] and would be delivering bad news instead of the Good News.

The Son of God's Beginning Message: "Repent for the Kingdom of God Is at Hand," Should also Be Our First Message.

God's message, revealed to us in human form[17] through His Son, Jesus the Holy One, is very simple: turn from your ways and **turn to Me**.[18] Biblically, we know that turning or repenting is the evidence of true faith and a belief in God. This ultimately produces obedience to God in a loving relationship. Through repentance, we replace our belief systems, our worldly thoughts, the flesh, and the devil's ways, as our minds are renewed by God's Word and by His Spirit. This believing in the mind and heart turns our behavior away from the way of the flesh to the way of the Holy Spirit.[19] This is what it means to *believe* in Christ for salvation.

Believing and repentance may unfold differently in each person, depending on his or her history. However, God's grace is truly

> Biblically, we know that turning or repenting is the evidence of true faith and a belief in God.

amazing as it will produce a life that becomes more and more like Christ.[20] His grace always convicts the real believer of sin, and reminds the believer of the righteousness of God and the judgment to come.[21] If this heart-change does not happen, self-examination is in order to see whether or not you are truly born again.[22] True faith in God is believing the Word of God and believing in Jesus Christ. Such beliefs will result in a changed and righteous life.[23] I am so grateful that the message of repentance was a solid part of my spiritual formation. People will often ask me, "How did you become free?" The answer is the Good News I share, the *Gospel Message* in this chapter, and the same message you will find in the Scriptural references below.

Paul's letter to Timothy makes it clear that the *Gospel Message* must be based upon the sound words of the Lord Jesus Christ, which conforms the soul to godliness.[24] The goal of this message is to mature the hearer into a pure love, an undefiled, clear conscience, and a sincere and devoted faith.[25] I rely on Jesus' words for leadership and filter all teachings through His words. If the message you're hearing is not changing your soul to godliness and setting you free from any form of lust-filled sexual desires and brokenness, you have the wrong message. Jesus said, "Narrow is the way that leads to life and FEW find it. Broad is the way of destruction and MANY will go on its path."[26]

I also rely on Jesus' statistics. In the parable of the sower, Jesus taught that only a small portion would actually bear good fruit after hearing the word of God.[27] Shouldn't we teach the same narrow way that leads to eternal life? If anyone—*and I mean anyone*—teaches otherwise, they are *not* teaching the Gospel of Jesus Christ. We should never teach people that they are justified to live in sin and an unrepentant life. This belief is completely contrary to the teachings of Jesus Christ. Yet, many leaders today teach such contradictions. John, Jesus' beloved disciple,[28] warns of this danger in his epistle, 1 John.

*"This is **the message** we have heard from Him and proclaim to you, that God is light, and in Him is no darkness at all. If **we say** we have fellowship with Him while we walk in darkness, we lie and do not practice the truth. But if we walk in the light, as He is in the light, we have fellowship with one another, and the blood of Jesus His Son cleanses us from all sin. If **we***

say we have no sin, we deceive ourselves, and the truth is not in us. If we confess our sins, He is faithful and just to forgive us our sins and to cleanse us from all unrighteousness. If **we say** we have not sinned, we make Him a liar, and His word is not in us." "**Whoever says** 'I know Him' but does not keep His commandments is a liar, and the truth is not in him, but whoever keeps His word, in him truly the love of God is perfected. By this we may know that we are in Him: **whoever says** he abides in Him ought to walk in the same way in which He (Jesus) walked." (1 John 1:5-10, 1 John 2:4-6). (You may want to replace the phrase with "we say" with "anyone says" and re-read. These warnings apply to all, even your favorite grace teacher).

John also reminds us of the importance of obedience in his Gospel, in the very words of Jesus:

> For God did not send the Son into the world to judge the world, but that the world might be saved through Him. He who believes in Him is not judged; he who does not believe has been judged already, because he has not believed in the name of the only begotten Son of God. This is the judgment, that the Light (Jesus) has come into the world, and men loved the darkness rather than the Light (Jesus), for their deeds were evil. For everyone who does evil (practices) hates the Light (hates Jesus), and does not come to the Light (Jesus) for fear that his deeds will be exposed. But he who practices the truth comes to the Light (Jesus), so that his deeds may be manifested as having been wrought in God." "He who believes in the Son of God, Jesus Christ, has eternal life; but he who does not obey the Son will not see life, but the wrath of God abides on him. (John 3:17-21, 36 NKJV/ESV)

Follow Me to the End

I shared the story of my conversion in February 1983. After praying with people who were completely surrendered to Christ, I was confronted with the Word of God in many ways, two of which I will share here. First, Jesus spoke to me in the power of His Spirit.[29] I did not understand what was happening to me at the time. My heart was pounding, and I felt very strange. I heard in my mind a voice I know now as the Holy Spirit. He told me that if I did not surrender to Christ, I was going to die. The fear of the Lord gripped my heart. I knew in my soul that I did not know Jesus Christ like these people. They spoke in terms of a relationship with God that I thought was crazy. They told me that Jesus answered their prayers, spoke to their hearts, that He was consistently known and felt in their home. I had never experienced Christ in that way, but I wanted to. They prayed with me to receive Jesus Christ as Lord.

Later that evening, in the car going home, my friend who had been with me and witnessed my surrender to Christ, asked me, "Does this mean you will stop being gay?" I told her I did not know for sure, that I wanted to follow whatever Jesus had for me. At home that night, I got out the big table-Bible, our only family Bible. Holding it my lap, I prayed and asked God to show me in His Word whether homosexuality was a sin. After all, the gay Catholic priest from my parent's parish had told me God loved me just the way I was as a gay man. God heard my prayer for truth and revealed it to me through His Word found in the Holy Scriptures.

Secondly, Jesus spoke to me through the Bible. As I opened the Bible, it fell directly upon Leviticus with the heading, "Laws on Sexual Immorality." There it was right before my eyes: chapter 18, verse 22.[30] It was undeniable that God detests homosexual behavior. Initially, I was angry. I could clearly see that I was worthy of death. However, I also finally understood that Jesus Christ paid for all my sins in His death on the cross, and that He loved me. He saved me from destruction and death.[31]

In the summer of 1983, we began to hear of a strange disease being reported by the news in Oklahoma City hospitals. At that time, the doctors were calling it GRID[32]—Gay-Related Immune Deficiency (syndrome)—or GRIDs Many of my friends, people who had seemed so vibrant and healthy, were now dying. In fact, more than half the people

> The fear of the Lord is the beginning of wisdom. Anyone who claims to declare the Gospel but excludes the fear of the Lord—the very beginning of wisdom—is immediately suspect to me.

I knew in the Oklahoma City gay community died within the next few years. In the midst of this tragedy, the fear of God instructed me and gave me life. God spared me and revealed His mercy.

The fear of the Lord is the beginning of wisdom.[33] Anyone who claims to declare the Gospel but excludes the fear of the Lord—the very beginning of wisdom—is immediately suspect to me. I look first to see if a messenger/teacher knows and demonstrates the fear of God as this is how the Gospel was presented to me by the Holy Spirit. Does the messenger teach that God is holy? Does the teacher instruct that we must turn to God in intimate relationship to become holy because God commands it? These questions must be answered with an emphatic "Yes!" We must respect the word of God.[34] Yes, we must know the Lord's kindness, but we also must know the severity of God, for no immoral person or idolater will be in heaven.[35]

Many times, I have been asked if I ever considered returning to the gay lifestyle. I decided in 1983 that I would rather live in abstinence than return to a life that clearly is against God's divine intent. However, I am married now with three adult children and three young grandchildren. I truly believe God's Word as it concerns homosexuality. I know He is holy, and I tremble when I think of the fate of people who choose to continue to live in immorality. The Scripture is very clear. ***No one*** who practices sexual immorality will go to heaven.[36] Yet false teachers, under the guise of hope and kindness, persist in spreading a message that is contrary to God's Word. Therefore, I embrace the words of Jesus Christ for clarity. (In the following passage, I have paraphrased in parentheses for the purpose of clarity.):

*"And **many false** (pastors) teachers will arise, and lead many astray* (they will tell you that you can be a "gay Christian"), *and because lawlessness* (the practice of sin) *will be increased, the love* (real love) *of many will grow cold. But the one who endures to the end will be saved. And **this gospel** of the kingdom will be proclaimed throughout the whole world as a testimony to all nations, and then the end will come." (Matt. 24:11-14).*

This is not a gospel of merely praying a prayer, but surrender to Jesus Christ as Lord. Will you endure to the end with me and the many others who will never go back to sexual immorality? We must endure to the end in a love relationship with Jesus Christ, who is the pearl of great price. Even if we live to be 100, this life is a mere vapor.[37] I will never be sorry that I embraced Christ, His word, and repentance from all immorality. Even if I am wrong, even if there is a remote possibility that a Christian could be gay, I have merely denied myself in pursuit of obedience. But, if the "gay Christian" or teacher of "gay Christianity" is wrong, the consequence may be eternal death. That's not a gamble I am willing to take. Are you? Even if you struggle with homosexual temptation to the end, if you deny your fleshly desires out of love for Christ, isn't eternal life better than hell? Isn't loving Christ instead of the world or our pleasure the better choice? No matter the temptation, Jesus is the better choice. Jesus is what makes heaven, HEAVEN!

Assurance of Salvation and Answers to Prayer

You can have assurance of salvation. The Bible is clear that we can have security IN Christ. If you repent of your sins, put your faith completely in Jesus Christ for your salvation, and continue in this faith in Him, you WILL have eternal life.[38] The promise is found in 1 John 5:13-15: "…to you who believe in the name of the Son of God that you **may know that you have eternal life. And this is the confidence**

> Jesus never taught us to say prayers to receive Him as Savior; He taught discipleship and lordship.

that we have toward Him, that if we ask anything according to His will He hears us. And if we know that He hears us in whatever we ask, we know that we have the requests that we have asked of Him." Unfortunately, there are doctrines and traditions of men and churches that communicate a relationship with Christ is achieved by raising a hand, or merely praying a prayer, or being a member, or being present in an organization. Jesus never taught us to say prayers to receive Him as Savior; He taught discipleship and lordship.[39] Although we should pray to receive Christ, it is not merely uttering a prayer that gives us an assurance of salvation. A devoted relationship, a sincere faith in Christ, results in righteous, repentant living and becoming His disciple. These are the biblical truths for an assurance of salvation. A sexually immoral person may have an assurance of salvation by praying a prayer, but their life must be accompanied by a sincere faith that produces a new life repentant from sexual sin. Giving an assurance of eternal life in any other case is not loving. The once-prayed, always-saved ploy in many church circles is a diabolical plot leading many to hell. It is a very dangerous teaching communicating that a sexually immoral person is saved. It is evil to lead people into a false hope. Would you like to be prepared on judgment day to give an account for having lead people into a false hope of salvation based upon the traditions and doctrines of men of merely praying a prayer? Would you like to give an answer to God for giving a message that actually sent people to hell?

What Will Be the Message? A Biblical Message or Man's Theologies?

Several church leaders[40] embrace the emergent, perverse grace message of "gay Christianity" and present a "gay Gospel." Their teachings are not based upon the sound doctrine of the Gospel of Jesus Christ or New Testament biblical instruction. Instead, they choose to embrace a false social gospel of a more palatable feel-good god and a man-made theology while they do good things under the banner of Christianity. Unfortunately, rather than embracing the Gospel of Jesus Christ, a gospel of self-denial that produces a Spirit-filled life of truly good works,[41] they embrace a man-made theology promoting homosexual "Christianity."

Which gospel message will you embrace? Will you follow a biblical message that allows the human heart and soul to be transformed by the Word of God or a man-made theology that allows men to live in self-centeredness and self-indulgence?[42] Shall we teach people that just praying a prayer and being a part of a community saves them eternally? Or shall we teach truth, that to accept Jesus Christ as Lord and follow Him in discipleship will result in a life of righteousness and ultimately eternal life for those who truly surrender? Which Gospel will you teach or follow?[43] The true gospel of Jesus Christ leads to life; or the "gay gospel" according to new trendy nice sounding words of "smart" men, influential theologians that leads to death? "There is a way that seems right to man, but the end leads to death."[44] Beloved, there is *no* "gay Christianity" in God's Kingdom or economy. Don't believe a lie!

Endnotes: (Please read the following Scriptures in context of this chapter:)

1. 1 Cor. 6:9-11, 1 Cor. 1:18, 2 Cor. 2:15, 2 Cor. 4:3, Rom. 1:16-17, 2 Cor. 11:3-5, Gal. 1:6-9
2. Jude 1:2-4
3. Rom. 9:1-3
4. 2 Thess. 2:3; 1 Tim. 4:1, 2 Tim. 3:1-5
5. Matt. 24:4-13
6. Acts 2:4-41
7. John 3:16-21

8. 1 Cor. 6:9-11, Eph. 5:1-17, Gal. 5:19-21

9. Eph. 5:6-9, 1 Cor. 6:9, Gal. 6:6-8, 1 Cor. 15:33-34, Rom. 16:17-19, 1 Thess. 2:3-4, 1 John 3:6-8

10. Matt. 1:21, John 3:16-21

11. John 14:26, John 20:22

12. James 4:4

13. Acts 5:32

14. Eph. 4:29-31

15. James 4:6-10

16. "The Whole Gospel for Gays" by Andy Comiskey http://www.stephen-black.org/blog/post/the-whole-gospel-for-gays-by-andy-comiskey

17. John 1:1, 14

18. Mark 1:14-16, Isa. 45:21-23

19. Gal. 5:16-24, Rom. 12:1-2, 2 Cor. 10:3-5

20. Rom. 8:29

21. John 16:7-9

22. 2 Cor. 13:5, "Born Again? Examine Yourself" by Stephen Black http://www.firststone.org/articles/post/born-again-examine-yourself

23. Rom. 10:8-11, Rom. 10:17

24. 1 Tim. 6:3-5

25. 1 Tim. 1:5-6

26. Matt. 7:13-14

27. Mark 4:1-20

28. John 13:23, 19:26, 21:7, 21:20

29. 1 Cor. 2:9-15

30. Lev. 18:22, Lev. 20:13

31. Ps. 107:20, Ps. 30:1-5, Ps. 40:1-5, Eph. 1:7-14, Rom. 5:1-10

32. http://en.wikipedia.org/wiki/Gay-related_immune_deficiency

33. Job 28:28, Ps. 19:9, Ps. 111:10, Prov. 1:7, Prov. 8:13, Prov. 9:10, Prov. 14:27, Prov. 15:33, Prov. 16:6, Prov. 19:23, Prov. 22:4, Luke 12:4-5

34. Psalm 119 is the longest chapter in the Bible dedicated to the importance of the Word of God in our lives.
35. Rom. 11:21-23
36. Eph. 5:5, Rev. 21:8, Rev. 14-15
37. James 4:14
38. Col. 1:21-23
39. Matt. 16: 24-27
40. Like the following: Alan Chambers, Randy Thomas, Julie Rodgers, Adam Hamilton, Jen Hatmaker, Justin Lee, Jim Wallis, Matthew Vines, Tony Jones, Brian McLaren, Rob Bell, Jay Bakker, Ray Boltz, Vicky Beeching, Andrew Marin, Troy Perry, Mel White, Tony & Peggy Campolo, Reba Rambo-McGuire, Gene Robinson & Neill Spurgin and the list continues to grow daily....
41. Gal. 5:19-24
42. 1 Tim. 1:5-7; 2 Tim. 2:14-19; 2 Tim. 3:1-5; 2 Tim. 4:2-4
43. Matt. 16:24-27
44. Prov. 14:11-13, Prov. 16:24-25

8

SHALL THE CHURCH SHOW REAL COMPASSION TO THE SAME-SEX ATTRACTED?

A Clarion Call for Church Leaders to Truly Love the Same-sex Attracted Person

"He has shown you, O man, what is good; and what does the LORD require of you but to do justly, to love mercy, and to walk humbly with your God?" —Mic. 6:8

GOD COMMANDS US TO LOVE one another, but how do we truly do that? It is only through the divine influence of the Holy Spirit living in us and moving us to love as the Lord Jesus Christ loves that we are able to fulfill that command and walk out such love. The Holy Spirit creates this kind of love within God's diligent, surrendered, and repentant people. He enables them to walk out love without denying His justice. Only in His love can we avoid the great compromise of our age. God looks all over the earth to find a people whose hearts are completely His so He can pour out His love and mercy upon them. (2 Chron. 16:9) As God pours out His love and mercy, this love manifests in Spirit-filled believers who embrace a holy lifestyle, freely loving others without compromising the holy justice our Lord requires. As His divine influence works in us, we are able to walk out a heaven-birthed love that reflects the real grace of God. Lest we forget, God gives His grace to the *humble* (James 4:6), not to the proud or compromising. His grace, and therefore His power, are given to those who put their faith in Christ alone. (Eph. 2:8-9).

How do we walk humbly?

The Lord showed us what it means to walk humbly in the example of His own life as He justly and consistently loved people with His great mercy. Only this long-suffering love, lived out through discipleship care and inner-healing ministry, can bring real transformation for people seeking to be free from homosexuality. A distorted and compromised love embraced by many church leaders across America will not bring freedom. Some leaders may believe it is kind and loving to empower the idea of "gay Christians" or to proclaim "same-sex attracted" or "gay" as legitimate labels, and identities, but they separate justice and mercy from love. This is tragic. Encouraging people to embrace a distorted image is not loving and is certainly not just. On the contrary, it is unloving, spiritually wounding, and could eventually be eternally harmful to souls. (Rom. 1:18-28, Cor. 6:9-11, Gal. 5:19-21, Eph. 5:5-6, 2 Thess. 2:10-12).

> Some leaders may believe it is kind and loving to empower the idea of "gay Christians" or to proclaim "same-sex attracted" or "gay" as legitimate labels, and identities, but they separate justice and mercy from love. This is tragic.

Same-Sex Attraction: Temptation, Lust, or an Identity?

"No temptation has overtaken you except such as is common to man; but God is faithful, who will not allow you to be tempted beyond what you are able, but with the temptation will also make the way of escape (freedom), that you may be able to bear it." (1 Cor. 10:13)

The mercies of God in His extravagant grace are deposited into the humble heart. God gives a way of escape to those tempted; however, He resists the proud. (1 Peter 5:5-10). Many today in the church, rather than wrestle with the issue of same-sex temptation and same-sex lust, argue instead that same-sex attraction must be recognized as part of a legitimate identity—orientation. Yet, there is no biblical basis for this surrender to LGBTQ+ pressure. This does not help anyone. This is the same demonic spirit that Jesus rebukes in the churches in the Revelation of Jesus Christ that tolerate the teachings of the Nicolaitans or the presence of Jezebel—it is a spirit of sexual uncleanness and perversion.

"We are human, but we don't wage war as humans do. We use God's mighty weapons, not worldly weapons, to knock down the strongholds of human reasoning and to destroy false arguments. We destroy every proud obstacle that keeps people from knowing God. We capture their rebellious thoughts and teach them to obey Christ." (2 Cor. 10:3-5)

A loving and just leader will help a person overcome lust as they teach them to take every thought captive. This was my spiritual formation as a new Christian. It was a fight. I am grateful that my first pastor, John Ward, taught me to forsake *all* of my old identity. A discerning and spiritual father will teach spiritual warfare to a same-sex attracted person. In so doing, he or she can walk in freedom from tormenting temptations. A Christ-led leader would never allow a disciple to embrace temptation or lust as a legitimate identity. Yet, this is what happens to many who embrace a gay identity or the identity of being same-sex attracted and call themselves Christian. They use ambivalent slogans of condescension and confusion, like "Is God Anti-Gay?" for the purpose of leaving the door wide open for so-called "unity in the faith."

Leaders who teach false doctrine mislead people into slavery to further sin and lust. Leaders who know the truth about what the Bible teaches on homosexuality but do not impart this truth to others, passively allow people to remain enslaved to sin and lust. No one in the body of Christ should have to live a life overwhelmed by attractions that keep lust operating in the soul. Love empowers the soul to overcome temptation; anything less is evil. Unfortunately, few teach the truth—that same-sex attraction is a condition of the soul as a result of our fallen humanity. Typically, homosexual attractions are a result of a distorted and painful history, which needs godly pastoral care and many hours of prayer with talk therapy. Many people who have same-sex attractions have been sinned against. They need freedom in their souls! Unfortunately, many today promote the idea that same-sex attraction is innocuous and a proud identity. This is so wrong, even evil!

> No one in the body of Christ should have to live a life overwhelmed by attractions that keep lust operating in the soul. Love empowers the soul to overcome temptation; anything less is evil.

There *is* a great need for ministry, love, and understanding for the homosexual and the person who is attracted to their same-sex. Most same-sex attracted people, with the longing hearts of broken souls, become consumed by lust as they deal with a wounded history, trying to repair a broken image. This attraction and its fulfillment through lust can never be the identity of anyone who is completely surrendered to the lordship of Jesus Christ. Still, many well-meaning church leaders promote the idea that being gay or a "gay Christian," or that being attracted to one's same-sex is legitimate or merely benign. They wrongly teach the idea of orientation and/or an identity, based on modern psychology and one's own sexual appetites. [1] This promotes *a false-self in fallen humanity* as something to be acknowledged. This deceptive teaching promotes distortion in the church and leads many astray with a false compassion.

Coining new and comforting terms, such as "mixed-orientation marriages" and other forms of sexual orientation only further strengthen the demonic strongholds in souls. Gay activists have browbeaten the church with words like homophobic, bigoted, intolerant, unloving, and unkind. This makes anyone who desires to be uncompromising in biblical orthodoxy subject to scrutiny and demonic pressure to be swayed into a man-pleasing spirit. After all, what sincere Christian is willing to wear the unloving labels cast on them by gay activists? No one! Reactionary leaders introduce deception, subtly legitimizing same-sex attractions and lust by their ever-growing cheap-grace teachings or by not teaching on it at all. Well-meaning, compassionate people are seduced by false teachings about grace and mercy, thus promoting a distortion of Christianity. This kind-license to sin makes an allowance for sins of the heart and mind to remain indulgent. We should show great compassion to all sexual sinners in the church, but these cheap-grace teachers align themselves with demons to turn the grace of God into lasciviousness. Some of them even joke outrageously about lasciviousness and mock grace.[2] "For certain men have crept in unnoticed, who long ago were marked out for this condemnation, ungodly men, who turn the grace of our God into lewdness (lasciviousness) and deny the only Lord God and our Lord Jesus Christ." (Jude 1:4).

The Grace of God Is Transformational

Flee from sexual lust and fornication for every other sin is committed outside the body, but sexual immorality is a sin against your soul, your identity and body. (1 Cor. 6:18)

The Apostle Paul used the word "flee" for a reason. Sexual sin is very dangerous and very damaging to the soul, and humans should flee from it as fast as humanly possible. Teaching acceptance of "gay Christianity" is equally dangerous. "Gay Christian" advocates teach lies; they are blind and deceptive guides keeping the souls of many in bondage to same-sex lust.[1] From these teachers we should flee. Jesus' way is to submit the soul through faith to His amazing sacrifice on the cross, resulting in righteousness. (Rom. 10:10). A true faith in God embraces inward holiness of thoughts. His divine call for salvation is to a new lifestyle of turning to Him for the joy of a deep intimate relationship with Christ as Creator. This requires us to die to all self-promotion of the fallen Adamic nature of the flesh (orientations) and its desires, which includes same-sex attraction, homosexuality, and all forms of sexual sin and brokenness. The grace of God is transformational.[3] He *always* makes a way of escape from temptation for those who are completely His. This is a litmus test to see if in fact you are truly born again: Do you desire to live purely in your thought life every day? Do you desire transformation? (See 2 Cor. 13:5).

We Are Created in the Image of God—Imago Dei!

As I have often written, we are created in the image of God—Imago Dei! The use of "sexual orientation" to describe a person's identity—such as "same-sex attracted" or "homosexual"—indicates viability for behavior outside of God's original intent for human sexuality. I have never agreed with the notion that sexual orientation—our sexual direction or desires—is equivalent to how we are sexually created to be. Use of terms, such as, "sexual orientation" and "mixed-orientation marriages" communicate a distorted truth based solely on human attractions and feelings, not on God's creation and intent. Modern psychology since the 1870s has provided these terms of orientation. Homosexual activism in psychology has legitimized more orientations. God gives us his only true intent for human sexuality. That is heterosexuality, a term also given to us by modern psychology. We are biologically and *innately* heterosexual by design. What we call *heterosexuality*, God calls *holy relating* between one man and one woman in a covenant marriage relationship with the potential to create life in His image through human sexual intercourse. God calls this relationship holy—two becoming one—a holy relationship that can be only between one man and one woman. This is Imago Dei. We are never more like God in His creativity as humans than when we are in concert with God in creating life.

> We are biologically and *innately* heterosexual by design.

One *cannot* create life through homosexual behavior. We are most like God in His creation when as *heterosexual* married couples, we produce children, also created in God's image (Imago Dei). This is the natural order, male and female. Although, some couples cannot produce, this is also a result of the fall as are those who are intersex. These people need great encouragement and our love to produce in other holy ways for God's glory. However, all other orientations are, at the very least, distorted emotional wounds from psychological (soulish) problems with their accompanying desires. Modern psychology, at its very worst, gives us sexual orientation as a way to legitimize sinful behavior. Under this diabolical plot, the orientation message can culminate the potential for mutilation of the body as we see in gender reassignment surgery. Of course, surgery never changes anyone's gender. This evil is very deceptive and tormenting for people. Humans are created male and female.

> Humans are created male and female. Heterosexuality is an ***innate created biological fact***, and therefore, cannot change. This is simple Biology 101. Any orientation idea given to us by modern psychology does not change the truth that we are created human beings, male and female at every level—Imago Dei.

Heterosexuality is an ***innate created biological fact***, and therefore, cannot change. This is simple Biology 101. Any orientation idea given to us by modern psychology does not change the truth that we are created human beings, male and female at every level—Imago Dei. Being human and under the curse of original sin, however, we have distorted attractions and engage in sinful behaviors. Humanity is fallen and, as fallen human beings, the *orientation* we have is a sinful orientation, not a sexual orientation. Stated simply, homosexual behavior and other sexual orientations outside of God's created divine intent for human sexuality, are sinful.

There Is Hope!

Jesus Christ came into the world to save us from all our distorted thinking. He gave us the Word of God, so our minds could be renewed by His Spirit, and so transformation could occur to the surrendered soul.[3] The Holy Spirit abides in those who put their faith and trust in Jesus Christ as Savior and Lord. Isn't it good news to know we do not have to be defined by modern psychology or our feelings, attractions, appetites or lusts? We are defined by the Creator, who created us in His image, to be like Him in a holy identity as man and woman, and we are created as His children. Yes! In fact, one can realize the lie of homosexual identity by changing one's behavior to live a holy and healthy life created in the image of God as heterosexual men and women—Imago Dei!

Realigning with the Words of Jesus Christ and the Holy Scriptures

The church needs a great revival—a revival to give justice and mercy to the same-sex attracted person and all sexual sinners. A revival where souls are truly transformed! We must base our outreach upon the sound words of the Lord Jesus Christ. We must give a genuine message of salvation, the Gospel message conforms the soul to godliness as I mentioned in the last chapter. The new ideas of outreach coming from church leaders are heartbreaking. They use the methodology of the world, through cute slogans and clever sayings, to lure same-sex attracted people with pleas of invitation and welcome. They offer no help in redemption, thus they allow the church to become an unholy place, devoid of transformation. They proclaim a message of grace where repentance is not absolutely necessary, just pray a prayer and have your ticket punched for heaven. This is not the Gospel of Jesus Christ.

"If anyone teaches otherwise and does not consent to wholesome words, even the words of our Lord Jesus Christ, and to the doctrine which accords with godliness he is proud, knowing nothing, but is obsessed with disputes and arguments over words, from which come envy, strife, reviling, evil suspicions, useless wrangling of men of corrupt minds and destitute of the truth, who suppose that godliness is a means of gain. From such withdraw yourself." (1 Tim. 6:3-5).

Jesus said, "Have you not read that He who made them at the beginning 'made them male and female'"—Jesus also said, "from the beginning it has always been this way." (See Matt. 19:1-10).

"It would seem that Our Lord finds our desires not too strong, but too weak. We are half-hearted creatures, fooling about with drink and sex and ambition when infinite joy is offered us, like an ignorant child who wants to go on making mud pies in the slums because he cannot imagine what is meant by the offer of a holiday at the sea. We are far too easily pleased."—C.S. Lewis, The Weight of Glory

This is the idea that human acceptance (mud pies) or a false identity, such as, "gay Christian" is worth more than divine holiness. There is a better way, expressed through the very words of Christ in Matthew's Gospel account and on the Sermon on the Mount. His words are very clear in confronting the motivations of the heart, especially in regard to sexual attraction and lust. The clarion call from our Savior is to present the beautiful truths of the Gospel for a genuine salvation and a biblical hope that brings transformation in these last days. His grace is transformative. It does not leave people with an out-of-control lust for as part of an unbiblical identity. If we compromise these truths, we do an injustice to the very people we say we want to help. Do not fall into the modern psychology trap of "gay Christian," placing the labels of fallen humanity onto people concerning their sexuality. It is not mercy, justice, nor love!

We should at least embrace an intercession of sincere love with great sorrow and tears as the Apostle Paul told the church in Rome. Read his words: "I tell the truth in Christ, I am not lying, my conscience also bearing me witness in the Holy Spirit, that I have great sorrow, weeping and continual grief in my heart. For I could wish that I myself were accursed from Christ for my brethren, my countrymen according to the flesh…" (Rom. 9:3) Yet the Apostle Paul's love—so profound—is willing to be accursed from Christ, willing to go to hell, so others would be saved! Most in the church are not weeping and praying, never mind willing to be accursed from Christ on behalf of another's potential for salvation. Rather, they are too afraid to call out how destructive homosexuality is to a person or to our society. How utterly unloving!

A clarion call and warning from the Lord concerning this day is found in Jeremiah 6:14-15 (parenthetical statements are added)—"The Shepherds (church leaders) have healed the hurt (deep wounding) of My people slightly, saying, 'Peace, peace!' When there is no peace. Were they ashamed when they had committed abominations (homosexuality—living in same-sex lust)? No! They were not at all ashamed; nor did they know how to blush (blush or show shame over abominations or sexual sins). Therefore they shall fall among those who fall; at the time I punish them, they shall be cast down,' says the LORD. Thus says the LORD: 'Stand in the ways and see, and ask for the old paths, where the good way is, and walk in

> Beware of thinking that the old ways of preaching the Gospel are not relevant today. You may find yourself as a false shepherd,

it; then you will find rest for your souls.' But they said, 'We will not walk in it.'" It seems these ancient shepherds have a lot in common with modern day influential theologians and church leaders of our day. Interesting as many have embraced psychology's orientation as being the very educated direction for same-sex attracted souls over the necessary deeper inner-healing of the soul.

Beware of thinking that the old ways of preaching the Gospel are not relevant today. You may find yourself as a false shepherd, not extending the call for holy repentance and a sincere healing of your own soul or the soul of the person who struggles with same-sex attraction or homosexuality. The Lord *requires* that we do just, love mercy, and walk humbly with Him (Mic. 6:8) as we bring souls sincerely to Christ in complete abandonment. ***"No greater love has any man than this, for a man to lay down his own life for his friends."*** (John 15:13). This is true justice, love, and mercy as we humbly walk with our Savior and Lord. This true justice requires a deep well of love, mercy and a lot of humble time in discipleship.

> This true justice requires a deep well of love, mercy and a lot of humble time in discipleship.

Endnotes:

1. The following promote "gay Christianity" and distorted perverted grace messages: Adam Hamilton, Alan Chambers, Randy Thomas, Julie Rodgers, Tony Jones, Jen Hatmaker, Wesley Hill, Justin Lee, Jim Wallis, Matthew Vines, Andrew Marin, Brian McLaren, Tony & Peggy Campolo, Mel White, Troy Perry, Rob Bell, Jay Bakker, Ray Boltz, Vicky Beeching, Reba Rambo-McGuire, Gene Robinson, Neill Spurgin and the list continues to grow daily....

2. You can listen to the audio of this message (Christian Audio Tapes, www.catapes.com, Exodus08-D Grace, by Clark Whitten). Notice that actual quote is edited out of this message. However, all of the laughing and mocking around the word lasciviousness on the audio doesn't make sense unless you had been there and heard Clark Whitten make this statement confirmed by several Exodus leaders.

3. Transformation of Persons with Same-Sex Attraction: Becoming Who We Are (Position paper on FSM website www.firststone.org/articles/post/transformation-of-persons-with-same-sex-attraction:-becoming-who-we-are).

9

PRACTICAL AVENUES OF MINISTRY TO COMPASSIONATELY REACH LOVED ONES

"Am I therefore become your enemy, because I tell you the truth?"
—Gal. 4:16

"And then many will be offended, will betray one another, and will hate one another. Then many false prophets will rise up and deceive many. And because lawlessness will abound, the love of many will grow cold. But he who endures to the end shall be saved. And this gospel of the kingdom will be preached in all the world as a witness to all the nations, and then the end will come." —Matt. 24:10-14

"Be on guard; stand firm in your faith in God, respecting His precepts and keeping your doctrine sound. Act like mature men and be courageous; be strong. Let everything you do be done in love, motivated and inspired by God's love for us." —1 Cor. 16:13-14 AMP.

WHERE DO WE BEGIN TO minister hope? There are generally three groups of people we encounter: the seeking, the deceived, and the "gay Christian." First, you need to be equipped to know theology and psychology to help in reaching out to loved ones. However, above all, I believe it is important to be completely surrendered to Jesus Christ as Lord and His narrow way that leads to life if you hope to help others find life. The temptation for many today is compromise, and it is unlike any day we have ever witnessed in our lifetime.

It is also important to understand the lies and false teachings surrounding homosexuality as you reach out to someone. I highly recommend the following resources to equip you. The first three were written by Joe Dallas. I recommend you read them in this order:

- *The Gay Gospel–How Pro-Gay Advocates Misread the Bible*
- *When Homosexuality Hits Home–What to Do When a Loved One Says, "I'm Gay"*
- *Speaking of Homosexuality: Discussing the Issues with Kindness and Clarity.*

I also recommend *Can You Be Gay and Christian? Responding with Love and Truth to Questions About Homosexuality* by Dr. Michael Brown. Finally, if you want the textbook gold standard on biblical teaching regarding homosexuality, Dr. Robert A. J. Gagnon's book is a must, *The Bible and Homosexual Practice: Texts and Hermeneutics.*

What I offer here is an overview of practical help. Over the years of ministry, I have received many requests for a simple list of helps for family and church leaders. This is not comprehensive, but I present the following so that you can see a list of areas to study so you can be equipped to be helpful in discipleship with the issues surrounding homosexuality and the church.

✓ Know the Arguments You Will Face—Deceptions and Lies
- Many believe lies. It is imperative to know what the Bible teaches about homosexuality.

- "Aren't people born gay?" (No). It is important to know the latest science.[1]
- What about genetics? Can you answer this question?[1]

✓ **Three Sets of People**
  - **The Seeking (Those who want change)**
    - » Christ in You—You are equipped because the Holy Spirit is in you. You do not have to know everything. Speak the truth you know that helped you to walk in freedom.
    - » They must be born again. If they have not truly surrendered their lives to Christ Jesus as Lord, they may first need an understanding of the Gospel.
    - » Patience in ministering to the history /roots—Study pastoral care, see the causes and roots found in this book in, *Overview of Homosexuality.*
    - » Long suffering / forgiveness / encouragement—You will need to be very patient. You will need to be encouraging. Forgiveness is a key to success for anyone seeking to walk in freedom.

  - **The Deceived (Ambivalent or Mocking)**
    - » Do you live a godly, uncompromised life? Our loved ones must see that we are the real deal. We must demonstrate a sincere life of humility. We lead them to Christ by our chaste and godly behavior.
    - » Pray—no condemnation (they are already condemned)—It is so important to pray that the minds of unbelievers will have the veil of deception removed. (2 Cor. 4:4).
    - » Wait on the Holy Spirit to open the door—use discernment.

» Don't make reaching out to your loved one about their homosexuality first. The Gospel must remain front and center. It is important to reveal to unbelievers or deceived people the truth of the Gospel first.

- **The "Gay Christian"—Religious**
  » Christ in You. You are equipped because the Holy Spirit is in you. You do not have to know everything! Speak the truth you know that helped you to walk in freedom. You may need to confront.
  » If you need to confront, do so with truth, kindly and wisely.
  » You must know and be equipped in the theological lies of "gay Christianity" and be willing to debate. Be able to ask the right questions and make the right appeals.
  » Know the Scriptures on this subject.
  » Ask questions about the Scriptures and the truth.
  » Be long suffering / patient / kind…. do not escalate. If necessary, walk away.
  » Are you living a godly, uncompromised life? If they can confront you about an area of weakness in you, agree quickly and walk in humility. You may need to ask for forgiveness. However, do not let them manipulate you in your kindness.
  » Be prepared with wise answers as you will be manipulated *(Remember the merging of the words "gay and Christianity" should never promote a victim status in the church, but in reality, it is defiling Christ's followers by putting homosexuality in front of Christianity).*
  » Pray without condemnation

» Wait on the Holy Spirit's leadership and pray for an open door. You need discernment, and a group of counselors to process with is always wise.

Practical Avenues of Ministry
✓ **Are you a safe person?**
- Are you a secret keeper?
- Are you compromising?
- Are you living a life of transparency and authenticity, one of discretion and repentance?
- Are you growing in holiness?
- What does your sin look like? Have you confessed your sin? Do they know you are a humble, broken, surrendered follower of Jesus Christ?

✓ **Demonstrate Real Christ-likeness**
- Expose hypocrisy in your own life. Demonstrate dying to self.
- Examine your own heart motives as you judge your own sin. Live this out before those who need Jesus.
- Strength in Weakness—Reveal the grace described in 2 Corinthians 12:7-10, by showing a life that never gives up, even if one continues to struggle for years.

✓ **Befriend a Struggler**
- Pray, pray, pray! Find ways to overcome evil by doing good to the struggler.
- Resist telling God what to do. The Holy Spirit might not go after the homosexuality first. However, remember that God is holy, and He will never leave a soul in sexual sin for long.

- Listen for the Lord's voice. Be prepared to help them begin to battle spiritually against their homosexuality when the Lord leads.

✓ **Jokes (Things You Don't Do)**
- Avoid identity-forming phrases or offense slang. (e.g. "That's *so* gay")
- Do not make derogatory statements.
- Repent of any cruel judgments. If you have done this, you need to deal with your own self-righteousness.

✓ **Do Not Say**
- "Love the sinner, hate the sin." as a way of continued discipleship. Saying this causes the gay identified person to believe, *"Gay is who I am."* He needs hope for a different identity that is truly Christ-centered. (Don't get me wrong, love the sinner, hate the sin is a right motivation, just make sure you are loving the sinner).
- Do not repeatedly call homosexuality a lifestyle.
- Understand that all the feelings and attractions associated with homosexuality are not a choice. (Yet the behavior is always a choice). (Remember, many have been sinned against in sexual abuse, and they are victims, but we need to disciple them to be victors!)

✓ **Honest Communication—Proverbs 24:26**
- Don't *demand* agreement.
- Communicate gratefulness in honest relating.
- Have compassion and long suffering, even when they are argumentative. This takes maturity. It is okay if you know you don't have the grace to handle it. Make it about your

inability to deal with the situation. Don't make it about them. Ask God for help and regroup. If you're a parent or close family member, you may not be the one God will use.

A Compassionate Response in the Church
✓ **Church Authority**
- Concerning church discipline, see Matthew 18:15-20, Galatians 6:1-3. When it comes to a place of dealing with a fallen believer, fellowship may need to be withdrawn. It is so important to never take the words of Jesus as a systematic way of fulfilling discipline for the sake of correction. It is important to be patient in the process of each step of Matthew 18.
- *"For judgment is without mercy to the one who has shown no mercy. Mercy triumphs over judgment."(James 2:13).*
- Err on the side of mercy in processing any correction.

✓ **Ministry to the Homosexual or Sexually Broken**
- **Are You Called?** We are all called to minister and serve. However, some are called to minister more directly. You need to discern your calling with spiritual authority.
- **Ongoing Ministry**
  » Know how to minister
  » Receive pastoral care/counseling training.
  » Participate in a Living Waters support group or attend a national training.
  » Understand mentorship/accountability. Learn how to do accountability well.
  » Gender affirmation—communicate the good of the masculine and the good of the feminine as demonstrated in love and longsuffering.

» Secretiveness empowers sin—There must be transparency in all our lives. Teach others consistency of confession and sincere repentance.

» Inner Healing—Pull up the roots by praying through the pain of the soul. Practice listening prayer and teach the importance of a vibrant, active prayer life.

» Navigate grief. Many times, someone coming out of homosexuality will grieve the loss of a lover or the painfulness of their history.

» Always point to the cross of Christ as a place of hope and healing as they seek freedom.

» Disciple their true identity—Who you are in fact from God's Word. (See chapters: The Overview of Homosexuality and Real Hope—How Freedom is Realized.)

» Know and communicate that they are created in the image of God. (Gen. 1:27 Imago Dei—male and female, not an orientation). See them how God sees them. (Read Ps. 139).

» Emphasize intimacy with Christ and other believers.

» Encourage them to seek healthy relationships with their same sex.

- **Practically Walk Beside the Struggler:**
  » Awkward Discipleship—for some, this means to know you are very different. You may not even understand their struggle, but you can still make the decision to walk with them in love.

  » Longsuffering—*Proverbs 24:16*—*"A righteous man may fall seven times, and rise again…"* We need to be there to help people in their failures. If they want to continue to follow Jesus and repent, there should be no need for shaming or continual, incessant correction.

» You are important to the struggler: People who have not struggled with homosexuality, "the ever-straight," are very important for the homosexual struggler. They help the struggler to see God's design as innately heterosexual.

» As an ever-straight, the struggler can see wholeness in you and gain hope.

» The struggler is important to you as you see your own weaknesses in dealing with a difficult situation. This is a catalyst for recognizing your own self-righteousness and your need to grow in love.

» Unforgiveness, unrepentance, apathy, rejection, emotional problems, and pet sins—there are going to be areas in the heart of the struggler that need much discipleship. You may need a team of caregivers.

Endnotes:

1. Charisma News, August 2016: *Johns Hopkins Scientists Offer Absolute Proof Gay Agenda's 'Born This Way' Is a Lie by Brendan Bradley* http://www.charismanews.com/world/59417-johns-hopkins-scientists-offer-absolute-proof-gay-agenda-s-born-this-way-is-a-lie *The New Atlantis—A Journal of Technology and Society—Special Report, Number 50—Fall 2016 Issue "Sexuality and Gender Findings from the Biology, Psychological, Social Sciences" by Dr. Lawrence S. Mayer, M.B., M.S., Ph.D. and Paul R. McHugh, MD*—http://www.thenewatlantis.com/docLib/20160819_TNA50SexualityandGender.pdf. This report conclusively reveals that there are no genetic links to homosexuality. No one is born gay. The American people have been lied to. *My Genes Made Me Do It! Homosexuality and the Scientific Evidence* by N E & B K Whitehead http://www.mygenes.co.nz ß The

Whiteheads' update the website with new and current science as it becomes available.

2. You can also go to my blog: www.stephenblack.org for the latest information as more develops.

10

FREEDOM REALIZED BY EXPERTS—FINAL THOUGHTS FROM A CLOUD OF WITNESSES

Freedom Is Realized by Those Who Endure to the End—
They Are Overcomers

"Without counsel, plans go awry,
but in the multitude of counselors they are established."—Prov. 15:22

"For by wise counsel you will wage your own war,
And in a multitude of counselors there is safety."—Prov. 24:6

THE FOLLOWING ARE SHORT, ENCOURAGING teaching summaries and testimonies from leaders with over twenty years of experience ministering to the sexually broken. They encourage us all on how freedom from homosexuality is truly realized in Christ. Each of these leaders have personally helped hundreds of people. In total, they have reached thousands of people and have helped them be set free from sexual sin and brokenness. Many souls are restored to wholeness through a sincere relationship with Jehovah Rapha, our great God who

151

is Healer and Jesus Christ our Lord. It is He who makes all things new! (2 Cor. 5:17, Rev. 21:5)

As you read through the following messages of freedom and hope, watch for their differences as well as for their commonalities. They differ in their manner of expression, their own individuality and vantage points. As with the authors of Scripture, these differences in expression and focus add to the authenticity of the message. This diversity comforts and reminds us that God has made "a mansion with many rooms" that accommodates us all as sinner saints on the road to full recovery and restoration.

Equally comforting is their unity and similarity. Over and over, in varying words, the authors will speak of the importance of finding freedom through stepping away from lies into the truth revealed. As one voice, they emphasize grace and the sin-breaking power of embracing the truth that God created us male and female. God defines us and not we ourselves. When we see and embrace that we are His image bearers, we start down a road of freedom and healing. All of these ministers point to the church as the primary means of application of the healing balm of accountability and comfort of boundaries which help us to press on towards the goal of godliness and maturity. Lastly, and most importantly, with one voice these writers emphasize that the spring of "living waters" is found only in a truly personal and intimate relationship with Jesus Christ. (John 7:38).

Get ready to be encouraged!

OUT OF HOMOSEXUALITY

Frank Worthen

ADMITTEDLY, HOMOSEXUALITY IS A COMPLEX
subject. Any Christian opinions are immediately challenged, and today
most see attempts to find freedom from homosexuality as futile and
counter-productive.

In my forty-plus years of helping people exit homosexuality and
end being gay-identified, I have formed opinions that may shed some
light on this confusing problem. Over one-hundred years ago, Sigmund
Freud saw the formation or root causes of homosexuality as twofold.
One: Molestation and Two: Arrested Development.

I have found that molestation is a contributing factor in about
one-half of the men I have helped. It is even more prevalent in the
women who have come through our ministry. Freud was a keen observer
of human behavior and even though more than a hundred years have
passed, many of his thoughts are still valuable. (Although I would not
agree with all of Freud or psychology.)

I believe that arrested development is a prime cause of homosexuality, but what does this mean? First, let me say that I do not believe in
constitutional, innate homosexuality. I do believe that the temperament

> I believe that arrested development is a prime cause of homosexuality,

we are born with plays a major role. However, I believe that from the point of birth, environmental factors are the major life influences in the development of homosexuality. Each person has their own unique life experiences, but there are some common denominators that are general in most cases. I believe that homosexuality is caused in part by a deep abiding insecurity in most. In testimonies of people with same-sex attraction, we almost always hear someone say: "I knew I was different from an early age." Security is built by affirmation in one's gender role and in most cases that affirmation was lacking. Other factors come into play, two major factors are: rejection by one's peer group and labeling and ridicule—that is believing what is being said by others when the name-calling and bullying sinks into a person's belief systems.

There have been many methods to change from being homosexual. In a few cases, the secular approach has had positive results. However, in my opinion, these methods have produced a dysfunctional heterosexual in place of a dysfunctional homosexual. I see no gain here.

It is my belief that only with the power of God can real change be realized. The first message of Jesus was, "Repent!" This message has largely been set aside by the modern church and deemed unnecessary. Yet it remains the starting gate. Repentance as the starting gate is the call to turn away from all sexual sin and idolatry and turn to Christ in a loving relationship. I am speaking of a genuine repentance that produces a new life of heart-felt sorrow and consecration. Avoid this gate and there will be years of misery and a consistent pattern of up and down

> I believe that homosexuality is caused in part by a deep abiding insecurity

victory only to be followed by failure. This causes many to give up and say, "God didn't work in my life."

I see the initial point of change to be a complete surrender to the lordship of Jesus Christ. Many who have come to me for counsel have wanted a method but often have been too prideful to break down and come before Jesus in complete brokenness and surrender. They resist the need to say, "I need Your help. I can't do this myself." Are there methods or steps to be taken? Yes, but they are meaningless without a personal relationship with Jesus Christ, who is the Healer. One such required step is a clean break from the world, secular thinking, and the gay-identified way of life. Many say, "Oh I could never do that! I have so many friends in the gay community!" Some may even have a gay relative. Yet, Jesus made this clear, unless you take up your cross, there will be no real progress. You cannot serve two masters. We have an enemy of our souls who takes unfair advantage of us and will use others to destroy the work God is trying to do in your soul.

Settling in one church and staying there is another step that brings the instruction and affirmation lacking from youth. Where once we felt we could not open up to a church body about our homosexual problems, today those in the church hear about homosexuality daily through the news media. It is no longer the "worse sin" in which to shun people. If there is an ex-gay group or an understanding ministry nearby, one should take every advantage of this group or ministry and receive the necessary help. It may take several years. Thank God for His work in your life and become involved in every way possible. These ministries and support groups are a blessing

> Progress depends largely on a grateful, thankful spirit. Through Jesus Christ as Lord, we can experience the transforming power of the Holy Spirit and His grace for transformation.

from the Lord and should be respected and supported in every way possible. Unfortunately, most of the time these ministries are sadly underfunded and overworked.

Progress depends largely on a grateful, thankful spirit. Through Jesus Christ as Lord, we can experience the transforming power of the Holy Spirit and His grace for transformation. With Christ, you will not emerge as a damaged, dysfunction heterosexual. Instead, you will emerge as a holy child of God.

Frank Worthen, one of the original founders of Exodus International, is fondly considered by most as the "Father of Ex-Gay Ministry." Frank was also one of the founders of the Restored Hope Network.

Frank Worthen went to be with the Lord Jesus Christ on Saturday, February 11, 2017

A Tribute to Frank Worthen and His Truth Squad—by Stephen Black

I was first introduced to Frank Worthen in Fort Collins, Colorado, in 1994. He was kind to me, however at that time he did not engage me. I was a new kid entering the circle of Exodus. Our relationship deepened later. Even so, I was struck by his humble manner at that first meeting. I had only a few encounters with Frank over the years, until 2011. I was introduced to Frank's first book, *Steps Out of Homosexuality*, soon after starting to work at First Stone Ministries in 1992. It is interesting to go back and see that many of the foundational truths in his book are repeatedly expressed by all the leaders contributing to this book. Looking over the table of contents in Frank's book, most of the principles of *Freedom Realized* are there. During an interview with me, Frank expressed some points we all agree are the core for freedom:

- It takes a fully committed person with surrendered motivation to find lasting freedom.
- There must be a complete surrender to Jesus Christ not only as Savior, but He must be the Lord of your life.
- You must be aware of the schemes of Satan and practice spiritual warfare.
- Knowing that homosexuality, at its core, is arrested emotional development and a broken identity, lasting change is only found as a process over the rest of one's life. Freed people are those who successfully align their self-image with the image of God. A life of growth in faith is found in a life of humble submission to God and His leadership.
- You must continue in a safe environment with a safe community of people. Therefore, most people need support groups and good Christian counselors to find lasting freedom from homosexuality.

In August of 2011, I called Frank about what I had seen behind the scenes with Exodus International. I was deeply concerned and grieving. He, too, was grieved upon hearing about Exodus' corruption and spiritual compromise. Frank was kind, yet authoritative. He laid out simple, yet profound guidance.

Frank was not surprised about Alan Chambers leading Exodus in the direction of perverted grace. He viewed Alan as a biblically illiterate, immature leader. In typical Frank Worthen kindness, he felt sad for Alan. *"Poor Alan..."* Frank said. He told me calmly, yet with great authority, *"Stephen, you have no other choice. You must put together a Truth Squad! You must gather leadership and confront the Exodus Board and Alan."*

This was the beginning of Frank Worthen's, Truth Squad. Whenever I called Frank, he was eager and available for counsel and encouragement. Frank was always about the Lord's work and furthering His gospel truth. We prayed many times together over the phone. In many of my conversations with Frank, we went over a list of people who might help in building the Truth Squad. I immediately started to make contacts. When Anne Paulk was apprised of what had happened, she immediately met with Frank and Anita Worthen to collaborate. Frank's Truth Squad was strengthened by Anne's skillful organization. When Anne went to see Frank, she said, "It was like a war room!" The planning had begun! The Truth Squad grew to be the founding committee of the Restored Hope Network. Frank gave his in-depth insights to everyone on the founding committee. He continued to provide input until the week he died.

In September of 2012, the RHN board was formed in Sacramento, California. This is where RHN had its first conference. I received the honor of speaking with Andrew Comiskey at the conclusion of the conference. I remember meeting with Frank before I spoke that day; I asked him to give me a blessing and an impartation. He was so gracious and humbled by my request. He was delighted and laid his hands on me and prayed over me as I knelt beside his chair. I was truly overwhelmed with gratitude. I asked Frank to pray over me and bless me every time I saw him in the last five years of his life. I believe the Lord gave me a very special blessing through his faithful servant, Frank Worthen's hands and prayers. Until the day we meet again, I will always honor Frank Worthen for his great work in advancing the Gospel and Christ's salvation for the homosexual. I will always remember his kind and dry sense of humor as he continually encouraged me and all the founders of RHN of the ministry obstacles. Frank told us to stay the course and to learn to delight in adversity. Frank knew if we experienced conflict, God would always use it for His glory! Indeed! It is all for Jesus sake and glory!

PLANKS OF RESTORATION FOR REAL FREEDOM

Andrew Comiskey

THREE THINGS COME TO MIND when I consider the "planks" of my restoration from homosexuality.

The first plank is a Spirit-inspired revelation of the cross of Jesus Christ, an exhibition of God's radical self-giving. In love, He called me to follow Him with my own little cross. It took time for me to grasp that revelation. Young and sexually charged, giving up "gay stuff" was hard. I knew deep down that my ways were destructive, but I had not had enough traction in the Christian community to discover the love that could surpass my sensational addictions. It took a couple years of volleying between two communities before I "got" the witness of the cross of love. Many people loved me and served as God's reminders that only Jesus could satisfy my desires.

Early on, I was just not ready to give up bad things. Whatever the issue, Jesus is faithful. He ultimately freed me to become faithful to Him. I remember listening to Handel's *Messiah* and when it came to the "Behold the Lamb" part, I fell down on my knees and wept. I

> Knowing I was created in the image of God brought light. The old ways were dispelled.

decided that He could have all my sin. I committed to seek to follow Him with my whole broken heart. I have not looked back since. As the blessed John Henry Newman says, "Ten thousand difficulties don't make a doubt."

The second plank involved the revelation that God created humanity as male and female. That is an unquestionable truth. However, my Bible-toting world stressed what you should **not** do sexually rather than promote who you are as God's gendered representatives, made in His image. That raised the bar for me on the need to make peace with my masculinity. I determined to face the business of rightly relating to women. Knowing I was created in the image of God brought light. The old ways were dispelled. People could no longer easily tempt me to find myself in fantasies of a gender "ideal" rather than to know that I am the Father's son, who already has the goods. My true identity just needed to be activated and owned. I needed to own my own masculinity. Gender reconciliation became a priority for me in my thinking and daily decisions. This brought about freedom that has resulted in my getting married. I have had good same-sex friends that need not be romanticized in my thinking, and I see people more for who they really are rather than being disgusted at their stalled development. Everyone has room to grow, to become who they really are. What freedom the Son gives us!

The third plank involved the church. I always loved gathering as members of one body with Jesus, our Head. I knew unless I was rooted in a dynamic community of faith, I would be sucked back into perverted needs for love. Besides that, I loved the real presence of Jesus in His saints, in the music, in the various efforts made to create a home for Him. As we gathered, He came over and over again. He took all of us deeper into authentic worship, which makes us more like Him. We are His image-bearers. Further, I loved how my pastors always made room for lay persons such as me to offer their gifts. This included an invitation for my wife and me to gather people with sexual issues. Together, we the broken discovered that dignity of His strength perfected in weakness as we sought to strengthen our fellows. Giving became the way we most clearly received from Jesus. In the same breath that we confessed our own sins, we could pray for others to be empowered to overcome their demons. What grace! My well-being is bound up in standing with the broken body of Christ (I know she is broken because I am a member!) and to help to make her beautiful for Jesus. These planks bring about the restoration of true freedom to be enjoyed as sons and daughters of the Most-High God.

Andrew Comiskey is the Founder and Director of Desert Stream Ministries
Author and Speaker
www.desertstream.org

WHEN FREEDOM RINGS

Joe Dallas

THERE IS ALWAYS A CELEBRATORY aspect to freedom; a ringing of bells and a gutsy, "Let's party" attitude. Freedom means release from what used to bind. A myriad of new options is the result.

I have had the joy of that sort of freedom. I have had the honor of celebrating it with men and women who want the same. In the process, three elements of liberty have shown up: the freedom to Recognize, to Resist, and to Rebuild.

Freedom to Recognize

Blindness to bondage is its own form of bondage; perhaps it is the ultimate form. After all, if a prisoner does not even know he is in chains, he will never so much as hope for something better. Since God intends liberty for His people (Gal. 5:13), He has a pattern of interrupting the lives of women and men by giving them the gift of dissatisfaction. Divine dissatisfaction is also a divine endowment. In our natural state, we would be content to go with the flow of the world, flesh, and devil (Eph. 2:2). In most cases, we recognize neither the flow itself nor its ultimate destination. Only by the grace of God do we realize there is something better and that we are falling short of it.

Freedom to Resist

> Only by the grace of God do we realize there is something better and that we are falling short of it.

Once we recognize what binds us and that we're created for something better, then we turn from it, hoping never to so much as think of it again.

This makes sense but runs counter to what we generally experience. What brought us pleasure or meaning at one time will, at some future point, beckon to us again. That is because repentance and mental deletion are two very different things. What we turn away from is, sadly, still lodged in our memory banks, and every so often those banks keep their doors open after hours.

That is what temptation is about: a desire, whether fleeting or strong, for something that gives temporal pleasure. Temptations are a fact of life in this fallen world.

While the presence of sin is a reality (I John 1:8), its power is history. Paul said it well: "Sin shall not have dominion over you." (Rom. 6:14) Clearly that does not mean it is non-existent. Rather, it means that now you are free to say "No" to what used to be automatic default.

Freedom to Rebuild

All of this leads to the freedom to do as Nehemiah did when he realized Jerusalem was in a decayed state. He recognized the problem, wept (while resisting the temptation to despair), then set about to rebuild.

For many of us, this can be the most significant part of the process: rebuilding damaged relationships, dormant potential, or personal ambitions long ago discarded. The freedom to rebuild is the liberty to say, "What was lost can be restored; what was given up on can be hoped for; what seemed impossible is now within reach."

> "What was lost can be restored; what was given up on can be hoped for; what seemed impossible is now within reach."

May every believer come to know this freedom and to guard against anything that would hinder it.

Joe Dallas is the Founder and Director of Genesis Counseling
Author and Speaker
www.joedallas.com

THE HEALING FROM HOMOSEXUALITY?

Anne Paulk

QUESTIONS ABOUT HOMOSEXUALITY ARE CURRENTLY the rage in secular and Christian circles. Can a person who has had gay feelings really experience change? Can they thrive? Is change of identity, thoughts, and feelings harmful? Currently, secular science testifies that feelings may change over a lifetime and heterosexual identity is the most stable of identities (Diamond, Savin-Williams & Ream, Kinsey, Regnerus, and many others).

But what about individual lives? Are people's lives really changed by degrees through the power of the Lord Jesus Christ in a holistic manner—in the realms of thoughts (identity), feelings (same-sex sexual attraction), and behavior (relationships)? We all know that significant life change is arduous; how much more in such a deep place as sexual desire! Because it is a deep place, men and women who surrender these areas to the lordship of Jesus Christ tend to experience great mercy and kindness from God, who transforms them from wallowing wayfarers to disciples who know their God. Although knowing God's kindness

> men and women who hold the hem of Jesus' garment are transformed into His likeness.

and mercy does not seem to change a same-sex attracted Christian, it is the key ingredient. Standing without excuses before the cross humbles a person and births new identity as son or daughter of God. From this place of very real tensile strength, men and women learn how to walk in ways that please their faithful Creator. (1 Thess. 4)

Rather than experience harm, men and women who hold the hem of Jesus' garment are transformed into His likeness. This occurs as they internalize His thoughts about them, which changes identity and behavior. When feelings of attraction arise for those leaving behind old ways, these men and women run to the cross and not away. They choose to not slink into the shadows but seek God's face and accountability with other fellow believers. When painful memories are stirred that give rise to same-sex attraction, these courageously bring their thoughts captive and obtain good counsel and prayer support where they experience the freedom found in God's heart for them.

Well-being and joy can be found at that same time as pain. Isn't that the paradox of the Christian life? "Whoever wants to be my disciple must deny themselves and take up their cross daily and follow me," Jesus declared to his followers (Luke 9:23). I consider those who surrender their sexuality to the lordship of Jesus Christ, "As for those in the land who belong to You, they are the great ones in whom is all my joy." (Ps. 16:3)

Anne Paulk, Executive Director, Restored Hope Network
Author and Speaker
www.restoredhopenetwork.org

JOURNEY WITH LIFE

Jerry Armelli

Acceptance

I SURRENDERED TO THE REALITY that through Adam and Eve, sin has contaminated everything. It has infected everything from the weather to our relationships; sexuality, thinking, bodies, behaviors—everything. I have let go of the false believe that sin did not infect my sexuality. It did! Simultaneously, I live in the reality that Jesus has provided redemption, restoration, and transformation. I have surrendered to these two realities: I live contaminated by sin, and I live in the power of the cross and resurrection of Jesus.

With that said, I am not in denial that same-gender attraction exists even in the midst of living heterosexually. I choose to be a slave to Christ Jesus—a bond servant. He has set me free from slavery to sin, thus I have chosen to bond myself to Him forever as a slave. As an act of my will, I choose to surrender to His ways. I deny myself to follow His divine design and intent for sexuality and relationship.

> He had a truth, peace, joy, and love that I knew I needed. I recognized that He was my Creator.

Divine Design for Relationships

I was lost. I was blind. I was in bondage to sin and brokenness. I had no resources within me to help myself. No one had the resources to help me...until I met Jesus. He had a truth, peace, joy, and love that I knew I needed. I recognized that He was my Creator. He knew what I was about more than I! I surrendered to His ways.

In His Word, the Bible, He told me how I was to relate to my parents, neighbors, enemies, men, women, children, bosses, nature, orphans, widows, the sick, the poor, and more. He described how He designed me and how to be in relationship with all people. He described His intent for sexuality. I chose to surrender to His divine design and intent for human relationships. His ways were going to be my ways. Oh! The freedom I have come to realize and know by surrendering to His will and following his design for relating! He has given me everything I need for correct heterosexual holy relating with both women and men.

Bread of Life

Food is good. I need it to survive. But even though I eat food and drink liquid, my life is sustained and kept alive by the words of our Creator. I could continue to eat and not be alive.

> "...man does not live on bread alone but on every
> word that comes from the mouth of the LORD.
> Deuteronomy 8:3b.

My life is alive, dynamic, transformed, and free by God's words to me.

"Jer' you are to reflect the unique expression of masculinity that I gave only to you."

"Follow me. I am the way."

"That which is unclear to you, Jer' I will make clear to you in time. Only live up to what I have already given you."

"Lose your life unto me and you will find life."

"In dying to yourself and unto Another you become like me."

God's words to me give me lasting freedom to live. His divine design and intent for me is: heterosexual identity, feelings, and behaviors.

Jerry Armelli, Executive Director, Prodigal Ministries
www.prodigal-ministries.com

FINDING LASTING FREEDOM

Jason Thompson

WHEN THE LORD LED ME to find hope and healing at Portland Fellowship, I entered with desperation for genuine and lasting freedom. I lacked any understanding of what was needed to find that freedom. To be honest, I hoped for some type of quick and easy fix. I was, in a sense, looking for the twelve steps or, better, a magic pill that would make my unwanted same-sex desires go away forever.

Many years later, I reflect back and see that the journey to wholeness wasn't at all a quick resolve. Rather, it was an ongoing journey filled with humility, prayer, suffering, faith, surrender and hope. Although at times it was extremely difficult, I am thankful that there wasn't a quick fix to my problems. A quick fix would have been incomplete, shallow, temporary, and never would have resolved my root relational needs. Even more importantly, I would not have experienced the depth of God's love and mercies through His powerful refining process.

Lasting freedom begins with our response to the Spirit's work. Confessing my sin, as difficult as it was, was the beginning of healing. The Lord exhorts, *"If my people, who are called by my name, will humble themselves and pray and seek my face and turn from their wicked ways,* *then I will hear from heaven, and I will forgive their sin and will heal their land." (2 Chron. 7:14 NLT)* I truly wanted the healing that God promised and, though not done perfectly, I sought to humble myself before God and others.

With this ongoing posture of humility, we lay ourselves open for the Spirit to search us. King David wrote, *"Search me, O God, and know my heart; try me and know my anxious thoughts. And see if there be any wicked way in me and lead me into life everlasting." (Psalm 139:23 KJV).* As God's Spirit worked in me, my false thinking, relational wounds, doubts and shame began to make their way to the surface. I had believed lies about myself as a man. I ran from trusted relationships and held too tightly to unhealthy relationships. I looked to the counterfeit to meet my needs. It was a painful process to allow the Lord to reveal the content of my heart; and what's more, I had to decide what to do with it.

Our continued response is that of surrender. When the impurities of my heart came to the surface, there was a temptation to push them back down, minimize them, secretly stash them away, or justify why I needed to hold on to them. As God continued to reveal things of my life that hindered growth in Him, I would practice the act of surrender. As I did this, an amazing thing happened: He provided me with excellent and lasting things! He repaired my masculinity, provided healthy relationships, and restored my true identity that can only be found in Him.

Lasting freedom does not begin and end in a season. It is an ongoing

> Lasting freedom does not begin and end in a season. It is an ongoing process of humility, prayer, and inviting the Lord to search my heart and refine and replace the old with the new. Again, I am thankful for a deep work of transformation and not a quick fix.

process of humility, prayer, and inviting the Lord to search my heart and refine and replace the old with the new. Again, I am thankful for a deep work of transformation and not a quick fix. Because of what the Lord has done and continues to do, I live freely in Christ and am able to know the deep love God and rest in His finished work each day of my life.

Jason Thompson, Executive Director, Portland Fellowship
www.portlandfellowship.com

THE FOUNDATIONS OF MY BEGINNINGS ARE STILL TRUE

Laura Leigh Stanlake

WHEN I ARRIVED AT A point of repentance in January 1990, it was just a "point" of repentance from immorality. That single moment of clarity about my condition before the Lord Jesus Christ did not vanquish the demons or win the battle. It seems that it was more like the door to my prison cell had been opened and before me was an unknown future.

I Put Away My Hiddenness

The first thing I remember doing was break my isolation and share my secrets with a trusted older and more stable Christian. This involved something like a moral inventory. The Holy Spirit enabled me to make a very complete list of all my moral sins. I confessed them to a Christian sister. I hid nothing. I told all. This accomplished several purposes. First, it put me in the position to agree with God that I was hopeless without Him and completely unable to help or change myself. Second, it gave me the opportunity to break vows I had made that kept me a slave to my impurity. Last, it fulfilled Scriptural commands: "Therefore, confess

177

your sins to one another, and pray for one another, so that you may be healed. The effective prayer of a righteous man can accomplish much." (James 5:16, NASB)

I Made a Clean Break

I believe that God prompted me to cleanse my home of all possessions connected to my immorality. I was ruthless in this area of obedience. It meant that all articles of clothing, all letters, all books, all gifts, all furniture, and all music that was associated with my sin was discarded or given away. Because I was a Christian involved in sin, this cleansing involved much of my Christian music as it was a reminder of my sexual history. This, too, fulfilled the Scriptural command to cleanse myself of idolatry: "Or what agreement has the temple of God with idols? For we are the temple of the living God; just as God said, "I will dwell in them and walk among them; and I will be their God, and they shall be My people," 2 Corinthians 6:16 (NASB) Also, "Little children, guard yourselves from idols." 1 John 5:21 (NASB) I put aside many friends and activities that were tied to my immoral activities and relationships.

> I put aside many friends and activities that were tied to my immoral activities and relationships.

I Sought Help with My Wounded Heart

Surprisingly, much freedom came from these two areas of obedience. I involved myself with people and began to build relationships with families in the church. I knew I had to get help with the root causes of my poor relating and sexual sin. I sought out a godly counselor and a support Bible study. These two additions to my walk with Jesus accelerated my growth and my helped me become more stable. A counselor provided constant accountability for the thoughts and activities that needed to be changed. I found a greater emotional health and more control over my mind and will. Thoughts and attitudes that needed my attention and the touch of Jesus were kept in the open, and I found ways of walking out my repentance. The support group helped establish me in the teachings of the Bible regarding the soul and relationships. They provided a safe place to talk about where I was in my walk.

Godly counsel helps me remain open and to discern areas that need work. I have relationships in which I can be bluntly honest—even when I fail. Consistency makes me stronger. These are the steps that keep me clean and free.

Laura Leigh Stanlake is the Director of Women's Ministries, First Stone Ministries, Oklahoma City, OK www.firststone.org

HIS STRENGTH PERFECTED IN MY WEAKNESS

Dean Greer

I GREW UP IN A culture that expected perfection. There was no room for failure. I was taught since I was a Christian, I should be victorious. Victorious meant no weakness, no trial, free from sin, and free from the temptation to sin. The truth was, I was far from all of that.

Isn't it ironic that the body of Christ is made up of those who have professed their need for a Savior but then spend their remainder of their days on earth convincing everyone that they do not need a Savior anymore? I have found, and truly believe, that this side of heaven I will need Him every day.

After my conversion and subsequent healing, I surrounded myself with others who were willing to be real. Those, who like me, still needed a Savior. We serve a God *who delivered us from so great a death, and does deliver us; in whom we trust that He will still deliver us.* (See 2 Cor. 1:10)

Within the Living Waters community, of which I have been a part for more than twenty years, we define "wholeness" by how well we manage our "brokenness." Brokenness refers to the damage done by sin; my

> I find freedom as I allow my Creator to name me rather than giving that authority to other created things.

own personal sin as well as the sins committed against me. Often, this includes temptation to return to the sins of my past or to exchange the truth of God for a lie as it relates to my identity in Him.

I find freedom as I allow my Creator to name me rather than giving that authority to other created things. Aligned with my Creator—the only one worthy of that authority—I live more from a place of integrity rather than living to meet another creature's expectations. As Andrew Comiskey writes:

Integrity means to be "upright, unimpaired, and undivided." We are all wounded healers. We minister out of the healing we have received. For many of us, that healing is fresh and dependent on our ongoing reliance on Jesus, especially in areas of need and wounding. So, to have integrity begins with admitting where we are still vulnerable in our motives and desires. We may still be broken. But when we admit it, we reveal that the real self is still in process. We do not hide behind the perfect testimony others may want to hear!

Choosing to live "in the light" in this way does not always mean I will never face temptation. It means I will be less inclined to give into the temptations that come. I know whose I am and place my identity in Him.

I have been crucified with Christ; It is no longer I who live, but Christ lives in me; and the life which I now live in the flesh I live by faith in the Son of God, who loved me and gave Himself for me (Gal. 2:20)

Dean Greer, National Living Waters Coordinator, Desert Stream Ministries
www.desertstream.org

SOMETHING BEAUTIFUL, SOMETHING GOOD

Jim Venice

I STARTED TO EXPERIENCE SAME-SEX attractions as a young teen. During my young adult life, I spent about seven years in active homosexuality in the early 90s. I had bought into the lie that I was born gay and had gay genes and was hopeless to do anything about it. I was very hurt and even angry at God for giving me gay genes. I would shake my fist at God and even curse at Him. I felt that He was unjust for doing this to me and then condemning me to a devil's fiery hell, eternally lost and separated from Him. In spite of all of this, He continuously pursued me! He would wait until I was alone. He showed up and knocked at the door of my heart and whispered, "I still love you and want you." In anger, I would respond, "I am mad at You; You did this to me!"

This continued until November 1996 when I found myself at an old-fashioned altar. I was very broken, bitter, and unclean on the inside. I had never intended for my life to turn out like this. I acknowledged how sorry I was for the mess that I had made of my life and asked for

God to forgive me. To my surprise, *He did!* I did not have to beg or grovel with God. He gladly forgave and cleansed me. I had forgotten how good it felt to feel clean on the inside. The Holy Spirit brought back to my memory a Bible verse that I had learned when I was a child: 1 John 1:9, "If we confess our sins, He is faithful and just to forgive us and to cleanse us of all unrighteousness." YES! This included my sin of homosexuality.

This started my journey out of homosexuality over the last twenty years. I came to First Stone Ministries and met my counselor and mentor, Stephen Black. Stephen helped me to understand that I had believed a lie and that I was *not* born gay with gay genes. He also explained that I was not alone. There were countless people just like me who were finding freedom from homosexuality through the power of the gospel of Jesus Christ. He further helped me to understand that there were legitimate unmet needs and underlying root issues that were fueling my unwanted, same-sex attractions. Only when these needs and issues were properly dealt with would the attractions start to diminish and eventually go away altogether. Until then, I would have to learn how to submit my feelings and desires to the Lordship of Jesus Christ.

> He further helped me to understand that there were legitimate unmet needs and underlying root issues that were fueling my unwanted, same-sex attractions.

Over the next several years, my attractions did eventually start to diminish and eventually go away. Today, I can tell you that I no longer consider myself to be a gay man, nor do I desire sexual relations with other men. I live a very satisfying and fulfilling heterosexual life. I am happily married with a grown son and daughter. I have allowed the Lord to use what He has brought me through to help hundreds of other men and women also find freedom from unwanted same-sex attractions. When I started my journey years ago, I was reminded of an old Bill Gaither chorus that rang true in my life: "Something beautiful, something good. All my confusion He understood. All I had to offer Him was brokenness and strife, and He made something beautiful of my life!"

Jim Venice, Founder and Director of Pure Heart Ministries
www.pureheartministries.org

LEARNING TO FORGIVE AS CHRIST FORGIVES

Shirley Baskett

WHEN I RETURNED TO JESUS at the age of twenty-nine, I wanted to completely leave behind the life I had been living as a lesbian for eight and half years. I did not think I was able to change, but what I did know was that there was no hope in the life I had been living. All I wanted was to be back in relationship with Jesus. I died to my old beliefs about where love and freedom could be found and was now at last willing to trust God, to obey Him, and to trust my future into His hands. The first key to my freedom and walk from this time on, was the recognition that no *person* could fulfill me; only God could do this. I was well aware of His forgiveness of my rebellion and self-will. Many of my attitudes had to be realigned. A strong first step was dealing with my false perceptions.

I had been very proud of my label of *lesbian*. It was my identity. God revealed to me the truth that

> God revealed to me the truth that my only identity was as a follower of Jesus.

my only identity was as a follower of Jesus. I had falsely thought that I had to try to measure up to the culture's portrayal of femininity and since I felt I fell far short of this, I deemed myself to be something other than the average woman. I was not interested in the things other women valued. I began to see that I did not need to be like them. Being a woman did not require me to wear makeup or pink lace. I was as God had created me, not some mistake, not a man in a woman's body as I had believed. I only had to be Shirley, the woman that God created. I needed to let Him develop me as the woman He had designed me to be. This was a big step for me, and all false labels fell off. I was not an ex-gay, nor a "gay-Christian," I was simply a child of God and a follower of Jesus. That was identity enough. Anything else would slow my progress toward making Christ fully Lord.

Other steps were a series of confrontations. At times, while I read a Scripture or heard a sermon, I would know that God was opening doors in my heart. One of the most formidable dungeons in my heart was a secret hatred for my mother. I had dealt with my obvious anger, my unhealthy perceptions of my relationship with her, and was well on the way to learning how to love her. Yet, I had held onto the "right" to retain deep resentment, and yes, hatred for her, until God shone His light into this place in my heart. I had a choice whether to argue and cling to it, or let it go and fully forgive as He had forgiven me. I have found that He will never force change. However, radical change can come if we let Him remove the baggage we have stored in our lives, especially unforgiveness. Forgiving my mother was one of the most significant keys to the freedom I have found in Jesus.

Shirely Baskett, Director, Renew Ministries, Melbourne, Australia
www.renewministries.com.au

RESTORATION FOLLOWS REPENTANCE

Phillip Lee

ON OCTOBER 5, 1985, I surrendered to God. I put my faith in Christ Jesus and embarked on a journey to become a godly man as I applied and practiced His ways. Some might call this process deliverance, restoration, growing into godliness, getting along, or moving from darkness to light. Regardless of the term used to express *change* and a new direction in life, I know I am largely here today due to three biblical and discipleship principles instilled in me from day one of my conversion.

Principle One: *Romans 12:2,* tells us we are to be "*transformed by the renewing of our minds.*" The Word of God is living and active and is designed to change us once we embrace and apply its statutes. The Bible is not just a book to read once and then sit down as if we were finished with it. A daily nourishment of the truth and authority of Scripture is imperative for any faithful follower of Christ Jesus.

Principle Two: I am responsible to develop my Christian character. It is through my disciplined and dedicated prayer life, faithful church

> When we do not use God as a means to an end but delight ourselves in Him, we condition our lives for many surprising blessings.

attendance, worship, and the fellowship of believers that my godly character is formed and sustained.

Principle Three: Finally, and the point I believe may be the most critical, is my pursuit of an intimate relationship with God the Father. When we do not use God as a means to an end but delight ourselves in Him, we condition our lives for many surprising blessings. God's Word promises that delighting yourself in the Lord brings about the fulfillment of the desires of your heart *(see Psalms 37:4)*.

God, the Father, is not just forgiving and merciful, He is also gracious in giving strength and power to those in need. Grace is God's empowerment and enlightenment that enable us to overcome our circumstances as we surrender daily and apply His Word as a healing balm. Today, I continue to apply these principles of discipleship to my own life as well as to the many I have the privilege and honor to mentor and disciple. Ultimately, resolving the need that drew each of us to a Savior will always be far surpassed by the valuable, useful, and honorable pilgrimage of knowing the Savior, Jesus Christ as Lord.

Pastor Phillip Lee is the Executive Director of His Way Out Ministries www.hiswayout.com

REAL CONNECTION, REAL FREEDOM

Dan Puumala

IN A WORD, I HAVE found in twenty-three years of ministry, that people find lasting freedom from same-sex attraction (SSA) through **connection**. I believe anyone can find consistent power to overcome SSA if they can attain and maintain meaningful **connection**: 1) to God through His Son, Jesus; 2) to a community of sojourners; and 3) to the truth of Scripture.

A simple note of clarification here: *freedom from* SSA does not necessarily mean the *absence of* SSA but rather *sovereignty over* SSA. When America declared freedom from England in 1776, England did not go away. For eight years, England resisted and we fought hard to gain our own sovereignty, which is the power to control identity and behavior. Nowadays, sexual orientation is no longer considered merely a part of a person, but rather a sovereign power which completely identifies or classifies people. It takes over a person's life. This conflicts with one of our culture's highest values, self-determination. As Christians, we voluntarily transfer our sovereignty to God, rather than to SSA, thus bypassing the issue of self-determination altogether. We submit or defer control of our identity and behavior to God.

Let me develop three keys to connection that set people free.

Intimacy with Jesus is primary. If there is no love of Christ, there is no motivation to seek freedom from other loves. Jesus knows and cares about each aspect of our personal lives. If we let Him, He will help us set our lives in order. He will fight for us against our enemies who want us enslaved to them or others ... anybody but Jesus!

> We must have holy, intimate connections with others.

Secondly, **we must have holy, intimate connections with others**. This happens when emotions are felt and shared. People need **healthy, intimate, non-sexual relationships with same-sex friends who do not struggle with SSA.** It is in the context of these intimate relationships that people discover their true selves—who God created them to be. We must be known by the church and in communities of like-minded individuals who support and help. Along with weekly church participation, we need therapists, support groups, and accountability partners in the church. One cannot fight for freedom alone and win; it takes an army! Simply showing up in these contexts is not enough—pulling into a garage doesn't make you a Buick! One must actually be known by supportive others as one who struggles with SSA. This is much easier said than done!

Finally, there must be a **strong connection to the Word of God** as the only rule for faith and practice. In contrast to moral relativism, we adhere to the Bible's absolute truth. Careful, thoughtful, serious study of Scripture and submission to its authority will change us. We renounce half-truths, cultural myths, and stereotypes. This establishes our identity on the foundation of truth. We become empowered us to stand firm in the face of temptation. The lies of the world, the flesh, and the devil have all been defeated by the truth of Jesus' Word. Jesus said it, "The truth shall set you free." Indeed!

Rev. Dan Puumala, M.Div., Pastor of Ministry Relations, Outpost Ministries
www.outpostministries.org

SURRENDERING TO CHRIST

Lee Preston

I REMEMBER A NIGHT I sat at my sister's house in Waco, Texas. The house was quiet, and I was all alone with my own thoughts. I wondered if God could and would truly save me. Could He really take the mess that I was and change me? Would He be able to bless me, take me to new places, and give me something more than I had found in my brokenness? The words came to my mind, "I can give you everything, but you must be willing to do two things. First, surrender. Second, seek Me with all of your heart to find your freedom."

To find freedom is an adventure of epic proportions. Imagine sitting at the base of Mt. Everest, backpack hanging from your shoulders and equipment attached to your belt. You stare up to the top and wonder if this is really what you want to do? The problem with homosexual sin is that it matches the brokenness in one's heart well. It is easy. Easy to exchange sex for intimacy, the created in exchange for the Creator, the immediate bandage for the complete healing. Freedom is a journey, not an experience. The things I learned as a boy, must be relearned now, and learning takes a lifetime.

> The adventure of surrender means that lies must be exchanged for truths.

Finally, true surrender takes true exchange. The adventure of surrender means that lies must be exchanged for truths. That which is temporary must be exchanged for what is permanent, and comfort must be exchanged for lasting change. The lies of homosexuality say: *You will never fit; you will always feel this way, and if you feel it, it must be real.* These lies are the shackles that prevent true freedom. Truth says: *You fit in the heart of God. You will not always feel your brokenness, and whatever your feelings say, does not always mean truth. Seek Me, says the Lord, and I will show you the truth and it will make you free.*

**Lee Preston, Founder and Executive Director,
Shadow of His Wings Ministry
www.shadowofhiswingsministry.com**

WHAT DO YOU WANT?

Bob Ragan

IN 1987, I REDEDICATED MYSELF to God after living eleven years as a gay-identified man. This time, I asked Jesus to truly be Lord **over** every aspect of my life, not just my Savior. In February 1988, I attended my first Regeneration meeting in Northern Virginia. What encouragement and hope I received by hearing testimonies of changed lives! It was impactful to learn and understand how my broken past contributed to my culpable reactions and laid the foundation for my sinful choices. My life verse became Luke 1:37, and I believe with God nothing is impossible. Nevertheless, I still struggled with knowing who I was and what I really wanted. I was too focused on the healing of my soul rather than the Healer of my soul. My process was more restless activism than Christ-centered peace.

The Holy Spirit took me deeper into Romans, especially chapter 6. Here He began to center me on who I am in Christ and who Christ is in me. I realized that my emotions, behaviors, temptations, or circumstances did not define who I was as a man. Acts 17:28 states that it is in Jesus I live, move, and have my being. Tim Keller says God is not after a morally restrained heart but a supernaturally changed heart. My righteousness is not based on a sobriety record, but on Jesus as my true,

> My righteousness is not based on a sobriety record, but on Jesus as my true, core identity.

core identity. With this understanding, my seventeen-year addiction to pornography was finally broken, though I still needed another level of knowing in my process.

Jesus took me to the Father. As I entered into greater intimacy with God as Father, knowing I was His son, my relationships began to change. God brought men into my life that accepted and walked with me. As I embraced my masculinity and became the man the Father created me to be, all my relationships were enhanced and made more whole. I related to men and women aright. I even began to experience attractions towards women. For the first time, I was drawn to the complement of myself as someone who was different from me! Still, even at this point, in my heart, I wondered what I really wanted.

In John, chapter 1, Jesus asks John's followers, "What do you want?" I sought satisfaction when my soul longed for fulfillment. The root of all relational and sexual brokenness is settling for false intimacy when our desire is for true intimacy. Our deepest, God-given desire is to know and be known by God and one another. Whenever I am tempted, the root is found in my drive for true intimacy; to be known. Will I choose the infinite, which will fulfill my soul, or merely settle for the immediate, which is finite? God began to draw me in a new way to the infinite. In 2008, I entered into a celibate relationship with my Beloved. This was not a compromise or acquiescent choice, but the realization I only had a place in the depths of my heart for Jesus. He revealed what I had wanted ever since the point of my conception. I continue to pursue my knowing of Him and becoming more like Him, as I walk on my pilgrimage towards home. And this, my friends, is real freedom.

Bob Ragan is the Northern Virgina Director of Regeneration Ministries
www.regenerationministries.org

RECLAIMING MY IDENTITY IN CHRIST

Michael R. Newman

EARLY IN MY JOURNEY TOWARDS freedom in Christ, God strongly impressed upon me to keep my focus on Him as the Healer and Restorer for my healing. My focus was to be on Him rather than the testimony of someone else. I recognized that I did not need to gauge my progress in comparison to others. This gave me space to experience my own unique recovery instead of looking to others to define healing for me. It also buoyed up my faith when others stumbled or failed, since my faith and restoration was not dependent on others success.

This has been so important through the years. Even as I have seen various casualties, I am unmoved. My confidence has always been rooted in the character of God, not the track record of others.

To realize that God's requirements for me in the sanctification process were no different than His requirements for anyone with any

> To realize that God's requirements for me in the sanctification process were no different than His requirements for anyone with any struggle was essential.

struggle was essential. I needed to break from victim mentality and feeling so unique and different in my sin patterns. Those were areas that had immobilized me and had kept me in my unhealthy patterns. I recognized that my process in overcoming homosexuality was no more difficult or problematic than any other sin issue, encouraged me to continue to move forward. As I acknowledged my deeper issues beneath the symptoms of my homosexuality, a more realistic approach to my journey was established.

A huge breakthrough was my recognition that I did not have to define myself solely on my emotions, feelings, and circumstances. Early in my journey, I looked to alleviate my anxieties and fears. I wanted to be happy apart from my same sex-attractions. I explored various theories, therapies, and healing techniques. I saw people stray from their convictions as they focused on their experience and focused on their feelings, which sometimes included areas yet unresolved. Somewhere along the line, it hit me that God's realignment of my sexual identity was not limited to my feelings and attractions. When I grasped that my identity as a heterosexual male was firmly rooted in His design and intent, I could rest in that spiritual reality instead of grading myself on fleeting emotions and feelings. This has given me the stability to persevere with confidence in my ongoing transformation.

Learning to enjoy the process as a lifetime adventure has been key. God has been gracious and gentle with me. He has accompanied me in progressive restoration in my life so I would not be overwhelmed by it. To recognize lies, eschew self-defeating patterns, and establish healthy ways to relate has become a restorative rhythm in my life. New, healthy, patterns take time to be established. Freedom is attainable with diligence. I have learned to be thankful in my weakness as I have seen God be my strength every day.

Michael Newman is the Founder and Executive Director with Christian Coalition for Reconciliation in Houston, TX www.ccrhouston.org

WHAT DOES IT LOOK LIKE TO BE FREE?

David Kyle Foster

FOR SOMEONE WHO HAS BEEN in the healing process a while, there comes a day when they ask themselves, "Am I healed yet?" or "How will I know when I'm healed?" What does it look like to be free? In that moment, it is helpful to understand some of the earmarks of what real freedom looks like. Seekers of freedom need to take comfort in seeing the progress that God has wrought in them.

These criteria are not meant to imply that there is a state at which the capacity to be tempted by a sin no longer dwells in us. Although I have tailored the following evidence of freedom to the issue of homosexual confusion, for the most part these criteria can serve as guidelines for anyone's path in overcoming sin.

1. Effectively keep perfectionistic tendencies in check.

Many people refuse to try something that they cannot perfectly perform. Since the path toward holiness is riddled with periodic failure, they refuse to give it an honest shot. Performance is tied up in their minds with God's love and acceptance.

A person who walks in freedom has learned that God's love and acceptance is based on Christ's work on their behalf, not their flawless performance. They have learned that God's love and acceptance can never be earned and can never be repaid—it can only be received humbly, as a free, unmerited gift.

The one who walks in freedom understands the learning process. Christ also learned obedience from what He suffered (Heb. 5:8), and grew in wisdom, stature, and favor with God and men (Luke 2:52). God's pleasure is not focused on our achievement of the goal. His pleasure is focused on our love-inspired desire to cooperate with Him as we move toward the goal. Those on the journey gain His joy in the relationship of the moment, not in some prospect of the future. A person who walks in freedom has come to understand this and is committed to putting perfectionistic tendencies to death when they attempt to re-assert themselves.

2. **When temptations come—consistently and quickly put them away.**

> The difference in a healed person, one who walks in freedom, is that they have had a radical change of heart and have acquired a higher level of discipline.

Notice I did not say "if," I said "when." You will always have memories of past pleasures and old mental videotapes of events that have brought great excitement and thrills in the past, no matter what the sin once was. The difference in a healed person, one who walks in freedom, is that they have had a radical change of heart and have acquired a higher level of discipline.

For them, temptations are consistently rejected upon arrival. They do not give them any time. They do not give them any consideration. In the redeemed mind and heart, that sin is no longer an option.

3. **When temptations come, effectively and efficiently turn the battle over to God on a consistent basis.**

The free person has learned how to allow God fight their battles for them. Long past are the self-righteous attempts to prove oneself holy and above sin. Dead and buried is the idea that we become self-contained, self-made entities of holiness. This person has learned that the only power over sin that is available comes from the throne of God and must be sought immediately and relied upon completely during times of temptation. They understand that without Christ, they can do nothing. They have come to terms with their dependence on God to keep them from falling and are committed to allowing Him to do His will of sanctification in their lives.

4. **The tyranny of thoughts and feelings has been conquered. Only minor skirmishes remain.**

A healed person who walks in freedom has learned that thoughts and feelings lie to us on a continual basis—that they are completely unreliable sources of truth—and with only minor and infrequent exceptions, (that happen to everyone during times of stress and defeat), no longer allow them to dictate reality.

When a soul walks in freedom, they have come to grips with the autonomic tyranny of thoughts, feelings, and emotions. They have learned how to assess and discern the true from the false. They have settled on God's Word as their only infallible source of truth and refuse to allow thoughts and feelings to be their god. When lies and emotions from the old life attempt control again, the healed person meets them head-on with the Word of God.

5. **Wisely and habitually guard heart and mind against whatever has power to resuscitate the old nature.**

Immature and unhealed people play games with God. They keep one foot in the world and one foot in the Kingdom. They engage in very cleverly devised games of self-deception, whereby they convince themselves that they must give in to one sin or another. They may consider their lot in life or their past brokenness means they deserve to be able to give in every once in a while. They convince themselves that a life of obedience and holiness is only for priests, nuns, and saints, but not for the average guy. They tell themselves that considering how far they have come and how much they have given up, God understands and approves of their dalliances with sin. They supermarket shop for holiness—in other words, they retain the lordship of their life as they tell God where He can make them holy and where He must leave them alone. Similar to shopping in a grocery store, they pick and choose what seems most attractive to them in the kingdom and reject what seems unattractive, thus they keep certain areas of their life off limits to the Spirit of God.

Anyone who truly walks in freedom has forsaken all such games, to the extent that God has brought these to their awareness. The rest of life is an ongoing discovery of the darker and more cleverly hidden parts of our fallen nature. The free person is set on facing those moments of truth and allowing God to tell them what to do and what not to do. In the process of identifying those elements of the sinful life that are fuel to further sin, they take seriously the need to eradicate such things from their life. Anything that may bring to life the desire for a sin is ruthlessly removed from their environment to the extent that it is up to them.

6. **Love for Jesus, born out of an abiding intimacy with Him, is now the strongest inner resource in the decision to turn to God to be set free.**

Love must become the single motivating factor for obedience. Any other motive is religion—is death. The person who walks in freedom has developed a deep and abiding love relationship with Him—the one who compels him to holy pursuits. When temptation comes, the central reason to turn away is the thought of hurting the Lord they love. This is too grievous to consider. During moments of intimacy with them, God has succeeded in writing His law on their heart. In other words, the desire to be obedient, to be holy, has become their natural desire and has replaced the previously natural desire to rebel.

Grace produces this fruit in our lives. Titus 2:11-14 tells us clearly that it is the grace of God that teaches us to say, "No" to ungodliness and to live upright and godly lives in this present age. Stated another way, it is in being forgiven again and again and again that we finally acquire the desire to be faithful to such a Lord. Therein lies the value in seeing is the darkness of our heart and our fallen nature. When God's grace continues in the face of that reality, our rebellious heart is conquered by such love, and we become persuaded that He has nothing but good in mind for us. We go from obedience to Him because "we're supposed to" (though not yet trusting Him fully) to obedience to Him because we want to (we trust Him completely). That makes all the difference in the world to Him.

7. **The mind, heart, and perspective of Christ is the consistent guide.**

Behavior associated with arrested emotional development has decreased considerably—such as magical thinking or fantasy thinking. Romance and reality have struck their happy balance. An understanding and appreciation of the complexity of life has blossomed. The self-centered, impulsive, impatient ego is regularly submitted to the lordship of Christ.

An intimate connection with God has grown to such an extent that you think His thoughts after Him, know what He is going to say before He says it, experience His heart for others, see things through His eyes, and have an eternal perspective rather than a temporal one.

8. Knowing Satan's schemes enables resistance from an offensive posture rather than a defensive one.

God has taught you how Satan operates and strategies to overturn his attacks. Your will has been engaged to such an extent that you now fight from an offensive posture rather than a defensive one. Knowing ahead of time what he is likely to do, you already prepare battle plans for every contingency. There are few surprises and even those are met with an aggressive relish for the opportunity to take ground for the kingdom of God, rather than defending besieged territory. You know well the weapons of warfare and value each opportunity to strike another blow against the enemy of not only your soul, but the souls of all those who are perishing.

9. A heterosexual identity is now the predominant one and is the one irrevocably embraced.

You use the occasional reappearance of the waning homosexual persona as a lever to catapult you back into greater dependence and refuge in God. As with the ongoing struggle between the old man and the new creation in Christ, you recognize old thoughts and temptations as a defeated foe merely trying to come back to life. You also recognizing that the only thing that will bring this foe back to life is your own poor choices. You understand the lie behind the old persona. You understand the destruction that it wrought, not only in your life and the lives of those around you, but also in the suffering of Christ. You are dead set against ever allowing these thoughts and temptations to resurrect again.

You have taken great delight in the formation of the heterosexual identity, and it is now the identity you have embraced. You marvel at and praise God for each new facet that comes alive. You are irrevocably committed to feeding the new man and starving the old man to death. The alternative is never even considered anymore.

10. When the fantasies of the old nature are temporarily embraced, return to correct actions is quick and with deep and true repentance.

In moments of discouragement, weakness, or carelessness, you may discover that an old fantasy has developed in your mind that has not yet been cast out. When this occurs, you use the opportunity of your imperfection to remember once again what Christ has done for you and return to Him with deep and true repentance. You use the opportunity of your failure to rejoice in the grace of God. You rejoice in your weakness and release anew God's mighty power to keep you pure. You keep short accounts—for example, each failure, no matter how large or small, is quickly countered with true repentance. Sin is not allowed to continue and condemnation over failing is not allowed to take hold. Instead, you run back into God's open arms as quickly as possible.

11. The focus continues to shift from self to serving others.

One major indication of growth and maturity is a shift from thinking of yourself first to thinking of others first—a shift from striving for what is yours to giving what is yours; an overall change from selfishness to servanthood. In fact, one of the best things you can do during your healing process (and after) is to deliberately enter into selfless acts of service—to give things away to the point where you actually suffer from the loss. Tithing is a helpful tool to start. Add offerings to it. Give away most of the clothes in your closet, especially the items you really like. Sell your car and go on a mission trip. Truly store up for yourself treasures in heaven as the Bible suggests. Remember, though, that such acts must be Spirit-led to be of value. To do them only to receive the praise of men will not cause you to grow at all.

12. There is a growing larder of "eternal fruit" in your life.

Following on from the previous point, a healed person has learned the difference between acts that produce eternal fruit and those that do not. They have learned to wait on the leading of the Holy Spirit. They have also learned that they must do so from a predetermined decision to do whatever God may say. They await His leading, His opening of doors, and His empowerment to move ahead. On the other hand, they have also learned to catch themselves when selfishness or laziness causes them to play the old "I'll pretend I'm not hearing God when it's something I don't want to do" game. In short, to a significant extent, what they do for God is done for His glory alone, not for theirs. At least that is the sincere desire of their heart. They no longer serve Him simply to earn His love or acceptance or as a way to pay Him back for salvation. Their love for Him is such that they cannot help themselves from serving His every wish. The focus of their life, both physical and spiritual, is no longer on them, but on Him, and as a result, eternal fruit is being produced.

13. Remnant behavior no longer misleads; there is no thinking something is "wrong with you."

In some ways, the healing process is a reversal of the process that created the dysfunctional thoughts, feelings, and behavior. In the early stages of the development of homosexual neurosis, it is purely an emotional problem. There is a search for completion or damage control vis-à-vis one's gender identity. Unless the child's life has been prematurely sexualized through sexual abuse or exposure to pornography, the early stages are typified by feeling the need to be near to or accepted by certain same-gender people who symbolize or possess the completion that is lacking in the seeker. There is nothing sexual about it. Early behavior is more a turning of the head, a catching of the eye, a staring at certain people, a feeling of exhilaration when they brush by you or acknowledge you. Sometimes it is a weird need to be near something touched or used by your idol—a piece of clothing, even sitting where they have just sat. Such moments bring a feeling of satisfaction, as though in touching what they have touched, a part of their sufficiency has been transferred into you. This kind of behavior was the first to appear and is often the last to go. Many people are panicked at its reappearance after years of healing, walking in freedom, and fear it is a sign they have made no progress. Actually, it is a sign they have traveled a great distance, and as they move on, it too will pass, at least as a controlling force.

14. Lastly—the bottom line: A healed person has learned one thing so thoroughly that they operate in it without thinking: knowing why helps, but knowing Him heals and is what brings lasting freedom.

David Kyle Foster is the Founder and Executive Director of Mastering Life Ministries and Pure Passion TV.
www.masteringlife.org

11

THE FIRST STONE MINISTRY EFFECTIVENESS SURVEY—FOR *FREEDOM REALIZED*

"Facts are stubborn things; and whatever may be our wishes, our inclinations, or the dictates of our passion, they cannot alter the state of facts and evidence."—President John Adams

Survey Introduction

THE FIRST STONE MINISTRY EFFECTIVENESS survey was conducted online from November 15, 2015 thru December 31, 2016. We started with over 1,200 intact client files. These 1,200 client files included data on people who were engaged with First Stone Ministries (FSM) over a span of 25 years (1990–2015). Initially approximately 500 people engaged and were invited to take the survey. In the end, there were 185 respondents and it took 13 months to receive all of their responses.

The main focus group for the *Freedom Realized* survey were those who pursued lasting freedom for themselves and who engaged with our ministry for at least one year in diligent pursuit of help. The entire

> Those surveyed, having been in the program at least a year, were considered those who made valiant attempts to resolve their childhood and youth conflicts, process gender confusion, align their life with a sincere faith in God and His perfect ways, and embrace a process of recovery.

First Stone Ministries Effectiveness Survey, a full published report with all the details and comments, can be located on the FSM website. You will need to provide proof of purchase of *Freedom Realized* to receive an access code for access to the full published report. Simply email: fsm@firststone.org for the code.

In detail, the main focus group for *Freedom Realized* are those who came to FSM with same-sex attractions (SSA) or considered themselves gay/homosexual. They participated with FSM to find desired freedom from SSA or homosexuality. To be included in the survey, the respondent would have had to have exhibited true effort and motivation. Those surveyed, having been in the program at least a year, were considered those who made valiant attempts to resolve their childhood and youth conflicts, process gender confusion, align their life with a sincere faith in God and His perfect ways, and embrace a process of recovery. For some, the recovery process required many years—much more than merely praying a prayer for freedom, as the gay activists cynically mock when they chant, "Pray the Gay Away."

Therefore, the focus group for this survey are those who truly met the criteria to succeed in finding lasting freedom or *Freedom Realized.* Information regarding these participants will come from the subset found in the cross-tabulation (CT) graphs and charts of filtered statistics. The filtering CT criteria are derived from the answers to the original two survey questions (SQ-1 and SQ-2). Those two questions address who the respondents are who have the greatest success for finding lasting freedom. The original survey questions (SQ) data is from all 185 survey participants. The data from those 185 participants are found in the graphs and charts marked SQ. The CT-filtered results will vary. Some respondents viewed questions differently based upon their own reality and current life experiences. Each survey question and the CT information has a conclusion statement. The final conclusion of the FSM Effectiveness Survey is at the end of this chapter. The following are all the survey questions as asked online, followed by the main body of answers. When comments in the survey are not included, it is noted. The complete body of comments will be in the full published report.

The Survey—from November 15, 2015 through December 31, 2016

Dear First Stone Ministries' Survey Participant:

Thank you for participating in this survey. The goal is to assess the effectiveness of First Stone Ministries' (FSM) offering of services of helping people live in accordance with a sincere and devoted faith in Jesus Christ as Lord. We are collecting information about participants in our ministry in their recovery from sexual and relational brokenness. The results will be compiled to show a picture of First Stone's work among those seeking help and the results will be published. We underscore the need for confidentiality in the ethical treatment of our participants and their information. Nothing of your identity provided by you will be disclosed to the public—it will be kept confidential.

Identifying You

1. **How long were you involved with FSM?**

   (please choose as close an answer as you can)

   a. Less than six months   e. More than two years

   b. Less than a year   f. More than three years

   c. Around a year   g. Other (please specify) _____

   d. More than a year

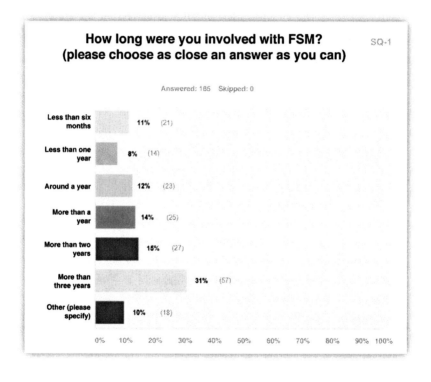

How long were you involved with FSM?
(please choose as close an answer as you can)   SQ-1

Answered: 185   Skipped: 0

Less than six months	11% (21)
Less than one year	8% (14)
Around a year	12% (23)
More than a year	14% (25)
More than two years	15% (27)
More than three years	31% (57)
Other (please specify)	10% (18)

0% 10% 20% 30% 40% 50% 60% 70% 80% 90% 100%

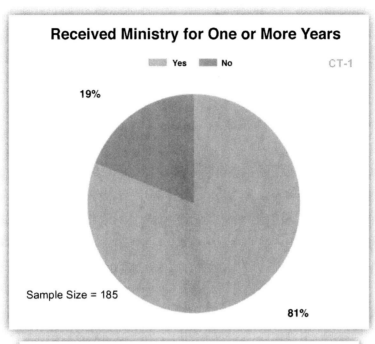

Received Ministry for One or More Years

	Yes	No	Total
Count	149	36	185
Row %	81%	19%	100%

Question 1 Conclusion: 149 respondents, or 81 percent of the 185 surveyed, received ministry for one or more years (CT-1). CT-1 (149 respondents) is main subset of focus.

2. **What brought you to FSM?**
   a. Sought help for myself.
   b. Sought help for my spouse.
   c. Sought help for my son/daughter.
   d. Sought help for a friend/relative.
   e. Sought information as a pastor/leader.

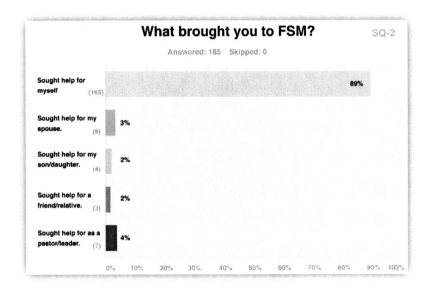

Question 2 Conclusion: The total number of respondents who sought help for themselves (as opposed to seeking help for someone else) was 165 of 185, or 89 percent of the respondents who are the main subset of focus.

Ministry Services

3. **Concerning the resources from FSM, how would you rate the effectiveness of the following:** *(main resources provided by FSM at the time of the survey)*
   a. USB/thumb Drive Library
   b. Literature/Articles
   c. Website
   d. Such Were Some of You Documentary
   e. Living Waters Guidebook
   f. Books by Andrew Comiskey
   g. Books by Joe Dallas

h. Media by Sy Rogers
i. Books/Media by David Kyle Foster
j. Books/Media for Parents
k. Books/Media for Spouses
l. Books/Media for Marriage/Pre-Marital
m. Books/Media—Other

Question 3 Conclusion: For brevity, the details of this question have been excluded. They can be reviewed in the full published report of the FSM Effectiveness Survey available at the First Stone website (www. firststone.org).

This question received answers from 181 respondents. The highest rated resources were: FSM Literature/Articles and the Living Waters Guidebook with over a 70 percent rating of Excellent-to-Good. However, most respondents were not familiar with the USB thumb Drive, the "Such Were Some of You" documentary, or the other authors books or materials. Less than 4 percent of the total respondents gave any of the resources a low rating. The conclusion is that FSM offers helpful materials and the majority of people who come to our ministry are very satisfied with the resources offered.

4. **Concerning FSM's ministry services, how would you rate the effectiveness of the following:**
    a. Discipleship/Pastoral Care
    b. Support Groups
    c. Teachings
    d. Seminars/Conferences
    e. Leadership Consultation

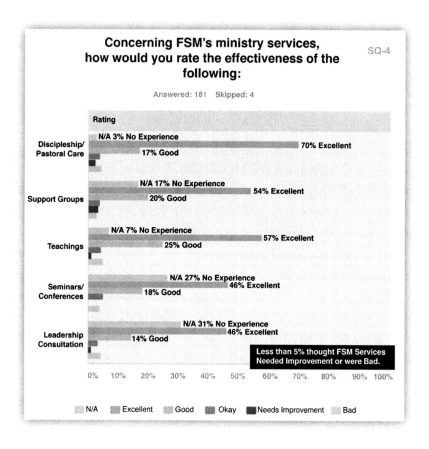

Question 4 Conclusion: Out of the 181 respondent responses, the services listed below received a rating of excellent or good, as follows:

- Discipleship / Pastoral Care: 81 percent
- Support Group Ministry: 74 percent
- Staff Teachings 82 percent

The Seminar and Leadership ratings were much lower; however, this may be due to the fact that 27 percent to 31 percent had no experience with our seminars, conferences, or leadership consultation offerings. The overall effectiveness of our services is rated excellent-to-good, with less than 5 percent of respondents communicating needed improvement or a bad experience. The conclusion is that FSM offers services that are very helpful, and the majority of people who come to our ministry are very satisfied with the services offered.

Pastoral Care Ministry

Concerning the following question, simply stated, a true follower of Jesus Christ has made Him the Master of their lives in believing and walking in obedience to the salvation message found in the Gospel.

5. **Do you consider yourself a Christian, what we describe as a true follower of Jesus Christ as Lord?**
   a. Yes
   b. No

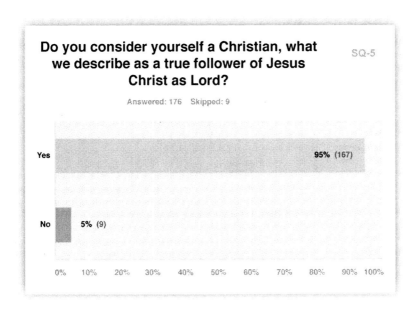

219

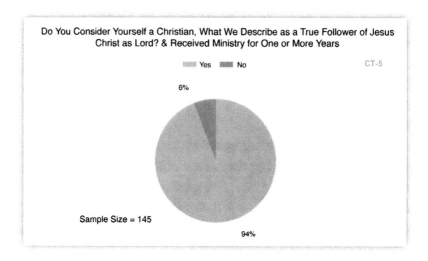

Do You Consider Yourself a Christian, What We Describe as a True Follower of Jesus Christ as Lord? & Received Ministry for One or More Years

Yes   No   CT-5

6%

Sample Size = 145

94%

Question 5 Conclusion: Of the 176 total respondents, 95 percent (or 167 respondents) believed they were true Christians. This is not surprising as the mission of First Stone Ministries is to work beside the church and help provide pastoral care. Nine respondents did not answer this question. The remaining 5 percent (or 9 respondents) answered, "No." The percentage changes merely 1 percent with the cross-tab filter (CT-5), which indicates the vast majority of respondents who sought ministry for one or more years were true Christians, sincere believers in Jesus Christ.

6. **If you answered yes to the previous question, did you make a decision to follow Jesus Christ as Lord after being involved with FSM?**
   a. Yes
   b. No

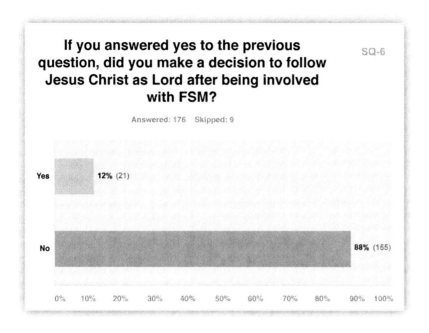

If you answered yes to the previous question, did you make a decision to follow Jesus Christ as Lord after being involved with FSM?

SQ-6

Answered: 176   Skipped: 9

Yes   **12%** (21)

No   **88%** (155)

0%   10%   20%   30%   40%   50%   60%   70%   80%   90%   100%

Question 6 Conclusion: The total respondents that answered SQ-6 were 176 respondents; of the 176, 12 percent (or 21 respondents) surrendered their lives to follow Jesus Christ as their Lord as a result of being involved with FSM.

7. **Of the ministers below, approximately how many meetings do you remember having with at least one individual?** *Answering: Number of Meetings, and Helpful/Not Helpful*
   a. Stephen Black *(87 percent Helpful Rating, 143 Respondents)*
   b. Cecil Claborn *(50 percent Helpful Rating, 8 Respondents)*
   c. Margaret Claborn *(44 percent Helpful Rating, 9 Respondents)*
   d. Andrew Franklin *(84 percent Helpful Rating, 43 Respondents)*
   e. Kim Gately *(67 percent Helpful Rating, 9 Respondents)*
   f. Steve Harshaw *(0 percent Helpful, 3 Respondents)*
   g. Mike Hawkins *(60 percent Helpful Rating, 5 Respondents)*
   h. Kim Hunt *(82 percent Helpful Rating, 17 Respondents)*
   i. Steven Hunt *(71 percent Helpful Rating, 7 Respondents)*

j. Jeff Janes *(91 percent Helpful Rating, 32 Respondents)*
k. Lezlie Janes (Brown) *(60 percent Helpful Rating, 10 Respondents)*
l. Chris Morrison *(89 percent Helpful Rating, 19 Respondents)*
m. Carol Palmer *(63 percent Helpful Rating, 8 Respondents)*
n. Lewis Palmer *(70 percent Helpful Rating, 10 Respondents)*
o. Laura Leigh Stanlake *(93 percent Helpful Rating, 74 Respondents)*
p. N/A *(40 percent Helpful Rating, 5 Respondents)*

Question 7 Conclusion: For brevity, the details of this question were omitted. However, they can be reviewed in the full published report of the FSM Effectiveness Survey available at the First Stone website (www.firststone.org). This question received answers from 176 respondents. Many of the respondents would have received ministry services from more than one staff member. The twelve staff members who worked for First Stone for two or more years received an average rating of "Helpful" from more than 80 percent of the respondents. The detailed reporting on numbers of meetings, respondents, and hours of ministry are in the full published report. The conclusion is clear, First Stone Ministries' pastoral care discipleship meetings for godly counsel and living were helpful to the majority people.

8. **Do you believe that meeting with the minister you named above was helpful for your Spiritual Growth?**
   If No, please explain why:
   If Yes, please tell us at least one thing but no more than three things that were helpful:

Number of Yes:	145
Number of No:	8
Number of Mixed:	6
Number of N/A:	3
Number of Blank:	23
Sample Size = 185	

SQ-8 Table

This is only a 5 percent sample of the total comments from SQ-7: Yes, No and Mixed: (for all comments, see the full published report).

Yes:

- "Stephen's own experience gave him a perspective that I needed to hear and was a valuable part of his being able to get through to me. He told me I was playing with fire when I had gone back to online sexual activity, and that warning has stuck with me."

- "His encouragement. He told me never to give up no matter how many times I fell. His testimony. Because he had overcome his sexual addiction, I knew I also would. His biblical teaching. I was always directed to the Word of God—and to source of that word—for my deliverance."

- "Laura Leigh Stanlake loved me when I was completely incapable of loving myself. I am forever indebted to her. The sexual issues in my life were like my addiction. Deciding I couldn't fix myself and God could and would if he were sought [she sought Him], were the steps to peace."

- "Laura Leigh Stanlake helped me connect my heart to Father God. Recognize truth that broke bondage. Walk out in wholeness & freedom."

- "They gave me perspective and clarity. Just as cars have blind spots, we, too, have blind spots. I was able to receive truth about myself, the truth that so often is marred by self-hatred."

- "The meetings I had with Andrew Franklin played a vital part in my spiritual growth. The most helpful thing that Andrew taught me was how to actively live in the grace of God and let the Lord meet me where I was at. He helped me realize that I didn't need to strive to try to be the perfect Christian to make God proud of me, but rather live in the truth, grace, and mercy that the Lord gives to us."

No:

- "No, this ministry is a disgusting institution trying to change people based on their sexual orientation."
- "No, I remember that I was upset with this guy who was my counselor, don't remember his name, but he was fairly new to the ministry. He said something that set me off and I decided not to come back since. It's been six years."

Mixed:

- "Helpful in that Stephen provided a very safe space for me to finally talk about my homosexuality. That was healing in and of itself. He was gracious and loving, and I am very grateful for that. Not helpful in that [there is] only one theological position re: homosexuality informed the teachings and the individual counseling sessions. There was no allowance for other theological, biological, or existential data that might suggest that homosexuality is indeed a part of God's design and is a natural, normal variation of typical sexual development for a very small percent of the population."
- "Most of these people were very helpful to me. Some have some doctrinal differences from my church, so they were not always helpful. Very loving, kind, and good at communicating the Gospel to people with SSA."

Question 8 Conclusion: For brevity, the details of this question have been omitted. However, they can be reviewed in the full published report of the FSM Effectiveness Survey available at the First Stone website(www.firststone.org).

Of the 176 respondents for SQ-7, there were a total of 163 that gave comments for question 8. (Therefore, there are many more to read in the full report). 145 respondents (78 percent) gave positive comments concerning their meetings with FSM pastoral caregiver. Eight respondents (4 percent) communicated negative comments, and six respondents (3 percent) had mixed comments. The conclusion is that 78 percent to 82 percent gave positive comments about their time with their ministers at First Stone. This conclusively reveals that the one-on-one ministry has been helpful at First Stone Ministries over the last twenty-five years.

Support Group Ministry
9. **If you attended any of our groups, in which group(s) did you participate and for how long? If you didn't attend, use the row for N/A.**
   a. Living Waters
   b. Summer Group
   c. Women's Group
   d. New Man Group
   e. Parent's, Family and Friends
   f. Wives' Group
   g. N/A

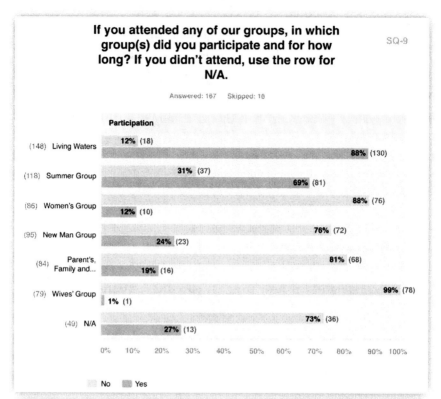

If you attended any of our groups, in which group(s) did you participate and for how long? If you didn't attend, use the row for N/A.

SQ-9

Answered: 167 Skipped: 18

Participation

(148) Living Waters — 12% (18) / 88% (130)
(118) Summer Group — 31% (37) / 69% (81)
(86) Women's Group — 88% (76) / 12% (10)
(95) New Man Group — 76% (72) / 24% (23)
(84) Parent's, Family and... — 81% (68) / 19% (16)
(79) Wives' Group — 99% (78) / 1% (1)
(49) N/A — 73% (36) / 27% (13)

☐ No ☐ Yes

# of Times   SQ-9

	1 time	2 times	3 times	4 times	5-10 times	11-20 times	More than 20 times	Total
Living Waters	22% 31	16% 22	12% 17	6% 9	14% 19	12% 17	17% 24	139
Summer Group	37% 33	19% 17	16% 14	3% 3	13% 12	8% 7	4% 4	90
Women's Group	65% 11	12% 2	0% 0	0% 0	12% 2	6% 1	6% 1	17
New Man Group	77% 24	6% 2	0% 0	3% 1	3% 1	10% 3	0% 0	31
Parent's, Family and Friends	45% 10	9% 2	5% 1	9% 2	23% 5	0% 0	9% 2	22
Wives' Group	88% 7	0% 0	0% 0	0% 0	0% 0	0% 0	13% 1	8

Question 9 Conclusion: 167 respondents answered this question. 88 percent participated in the FSM's, Living Waters group (runs approximately 28-30 weeks at a time). 69 percent participated in FSM's Summer Group, and the other groups can be seen above. Of the majority of those who are successful in finding lasting freedom, 66 percent to 88 percent participate in FSM's Living Waters, which is an intensive support group environment that provides real answers and a safe place to confess sin(s) weekly and receive prayer covering. The other support groups also provide the same type of prayer ministry, but in a shorter time-frame, generally 8-12 weeks.

10. **If you participated in the Living Waters program, did you complete at least 90 percent of the program?**
    k. Yes
    l. No
    m. N/A

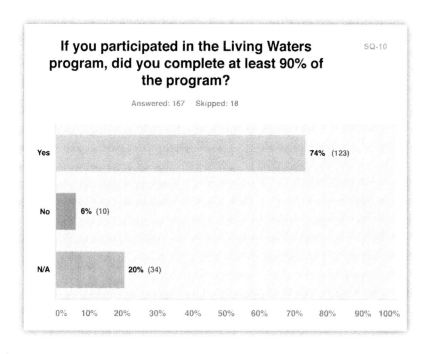

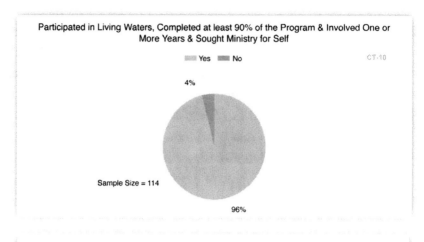

Participated in Living Waters, Completed at least 90% of the Program & Involved One or More Years & Sought Ministry for Self

Yes ▓ No

CT-10

4%

Sample Size = 114

96%

Participated in the Living Waters Program, Completed at least 90% of the Program & Involved One or More Years & Sought Ministry for Self

	Yes	No	Total
Count	109	5	114
Row %	96%	4%	100%

Question 10 Conclusion: The majority of respondents, 96 percent, participated in FSM's Living Waters for more than 90 percent of the meetings. These respondents were involved with FSM for more than one year. The overall conclusion is that those who have lasting freedom have consistently participated in support group ministry.

11. **Do you believe that the support group you participated in was helpful for your spiritual growth?** *(Comments were received for this question)*
    a. Yes
    b. No
    c. N/A

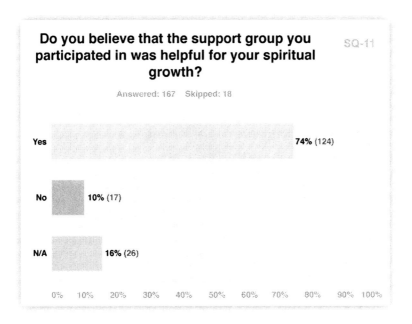

Do you believe that the support group you participated in was helpful for your spiritual growth?

SQ-11

Answered: 167   Skipped: 18

Yes — **74%** (124)

No — **10%** (17)

N/A — **16%** (26)

0% 10% 20% 30% 40% 50% 60% 70% 80% 90% 100%

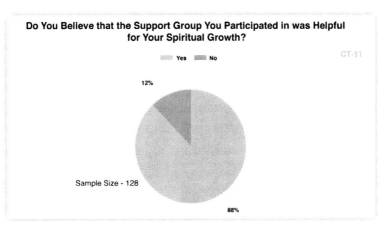

Do You Believe that the Support Group You Participated in was Helpful for Your Spiritual Growth?

Yes   No

CT-11

12%

Sample Size - 128

88%

Do You Believe that the Support Group You Participated in was Helpful for Your Spiritual Growth? & Received Ministry for One or More Years

	Yes	No	Total
Count	113	15	128
Row %	88 %	12%	100%

229

Comments were received for Question 11. A 5 percent Sample of the total responses from SQ-11: Yes, No and Mixed: (for all comments, see full published report).

Yes:

- "I appreciated the times when I moved to the middle of the circle and everyone came around me, laid hands on me and prayed. Those were powerful. I also appreciated that we could be very open with our struggles. I appreciated feedback I received from others in the group."

- "It was all geared for ministry to men and women with SSA like myself. I saw a number of people 'go back out there' but just as many chose to follow closely to Jesus."

- "It was a chance to visit openly without fear of condemnation. I was challenged as to why I was there. Was I being real or just there for outward appearance?"

- "Living Waters helped me to understand how I ended up with such relational brokenness. In understanding the hows, God healed hurts and gave me freedom!"

- "Living Waters is an exceptional group where I learned so much about myself. I felt very comfortable about being able to open up about the circumstances surrounding my life and knew that is exactly where the Lord had led me to be. The staff and volunteers were extremely understanding and helpful."

No:

- "I'm gay, and I was always skeptical that you all could 'fix' me."

Mixed:

- "First I want to clarify that I may not have completed 90 percent of the Living Waters program. I'm just not sure.... This is a tough one to answer. 'Yes' in that it provided a safe space to finally talk about my sexuality and my conflicted feelings around homosexuality. 'No' because the underlying theological position of the program (i.e. homosexuality is sinful and not part of God's design) is flawed."

Number of Yes:	98	SQ-11 Table
Number of No:	5	
Number of Mixed:	5	
Number of N/A:	15	
Number of Blank:	62	
Sample Size = 185		

Question 11 Conclusion: 88 percent of those who were in FSM's *Living Waters* were also respondents who received at least one year of ministry with FSM. 90 percent (98 respondents) gave positive comments, only five respondents (4 percent) gave negative comments, and another five respondents (4 percent) gave mixed comments. Another sample of more comments from the follow-up SQ-12 are below.

12. Based upon your response to the previous question:
If No, please explain why you felt it was not helpful. If Yes, please tell us at least one thing but no more than three things that were helpful:

Number of Yes:	101	SQ-12 Table
Number of No:	4	
Number of Mixed:	4	
Number of N/A:	16	
Number of Blank:	60	
Sample Size = 185		

A 5 percent sample of the total responses from SQ-12: Yes, No and Mixed: (for all comments, see full published report).

Yes:
- "Overcoming judgments, recognizing our need for the CROSS daily, and love my wife more sincerely."
- "It was helpful to be able to talk to others about my addiction. Gain encouragement that I could succeed."
- "The smaller group sessions were beneficial in knowing I was not alone in this struggle and seeing others become more free was an encouragement, too. The large group settings were beneficial in allowing members to worship together and the teachings from Stephen and Laura Leigh strengthened my hope."
- "Being able to talk with others about their struggles and hearing that I am not alone. Recognizing and writing down my own sinful attitudes. Being able to help others, too."
- "Yes, everything about FSM is life changing for me. I finally have hope to be married and have the family I have always wanted."

No:
- "Because it's not unbiblical to be gay. That's what you guys can't get through your heads. You're trying to alter someone's own person who was made in the image of God."

Mixed:
- "This is a tough one to answer. 'Yes' in that it provided a safe space to finally talk about my sexuality and my conflicted feelings around homosexuality. 'No' because the underlying theological position of the program (i.e. homosexuality is sinful and not part of God's design) is flawed."

Question 12 Conclusion: 88 percent of those who were in FSM's *Living Waters* were also respondents who received at least one year of ministry. 98 respondents (52 percent of the total) gave positive comments. Only five respondents (2 percent) gave negative comments, and another five respondents (2 percent) gave mixed comments. 101 respondents gave positive, life-changing comments on SQ12. The conclusion is that the majority of respondents gave endorsing comments concerning their time in the support group programs offered by First Stone Ministries.

Sexual and Relational Brokenness

13. **Did you come to FSM having same-sex attractions?**

    a. Yes

    b. No

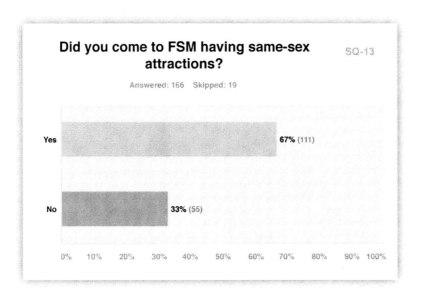

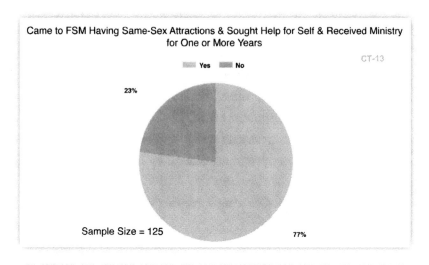

Came to FSM Having Same-Sex Attractions & Sought Help for Self & Received Ministry for One or More Years

CT-13

Yes   No

23%

77%

Sample Size = 125

Came to FSM Having Same-Sex Attractions & Sought Ministry for Self & Received Ministry for One or More Years

	Yes	No	Total
Count	96	29	125
Row %	77%	23%	100%

Question 13 Conclusion:

67 percent or 111 respondents of the entire survey SQ-13 answered "Yes" they came to FSM due to same-sex attraction. Of the 33 percent (or 55 respondents) that answered "No", 19 respondents did not answer the question. Applying the CT-13 filter reveals 77 percent (or 96 respondents) had same-sex attractions.

14. **If your answer to question 13 was Yes or No, did you consider yourself a homosexual upon coming to FSM?**
    a. Yes
    b. No
    c. N/A

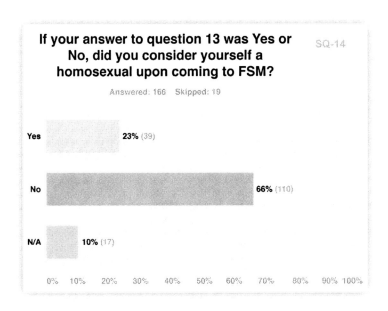

If your answer to question 13 was Yes or No, did you consider yourself a homosexual upon coming to FSM?

SQ-14

Answered: 166   Skipped: 19

Yes   23% (39)

No   66% (110)

N/A   10% (17)

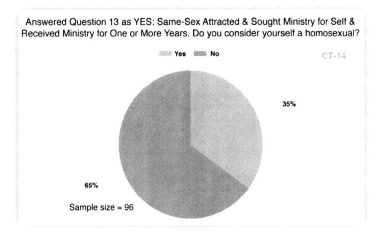

Answered Question 13 as YES: Same-Sex Attracted & Sought Ministry for Self & Received Ministry for One or More Years. Do you consider yourself a homosexual?

Yes   No

CT-14

35%

65%

Sample size = 96

Answered Question 13 as YES: Same-Sex Attracted & Sought Ministry for Self & Received Ministry for One or More Years. Do you consider yourself a homosexual?

	Yes	No	Total
Count	34	62	96
Row %	35%	65%	100%

235

Question 14 Conclusion:

The overall survey question, SQ-14, revealed that 66 percent of the 185 respondents came to FSM with same-sex attractions but did not consider themselves a homosexual. 23 percent said yes, they were homosexuals. Of those who received one year or more of ministry and who sought help for themselves, 65 percent of the respondents did not consider themselves to be homosexual. This is only a 1 percent change, yet 35 percent of this latter group did consider themselves homosexual.

15. **Pertaining to question 13, if you answered Yes or No, please select the best response: "I considered myself as"**
   a. same-sex attracted but not homosexual
   b. heterosexual
   c. bi-sexual
   d. asexual
   e. transgender
   f. intersex

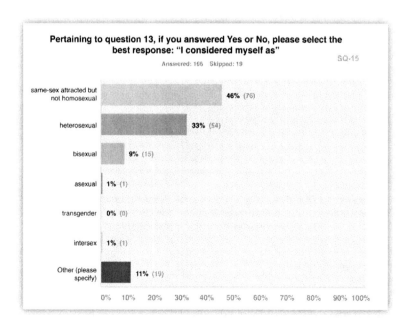

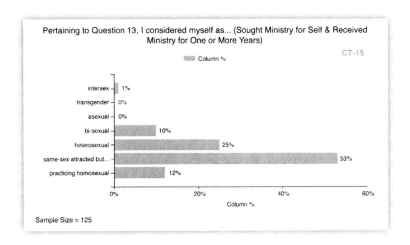

Pertaining to Question 13, I considered myself as... (Sought Ministry for Self & Received Ministry for One or More Years)

CT-15

Sample Size = 125

CT-15

Pertaining to Question 13, I considered myself as... (Sought Ministry for Self & Received Ministry for One or More Years)

		Total
	Sample Size	125
practicing homosexual		
	Count	15
	Column %	12%
same-sex attracted but not homosexual		
	Count	66
	Column %	53%
heterosexual		
	Count	31
	Column %	25%
bi-sexual		
	Count	
	Column %	10%
asexual		
	Count	0
	Column %	0%
transgender		
	Count	0
	Column %	0%
intersex		
	Count	1
	Column %	1%

237

Question 15 Conclusion: Of the respondents who participated for one or more years and sought help for themselves: 12 percent were practicing homosexuals, 53 percent had same-sex attractions but did not consider themselves homosexual or gay, and another 10 percent considered themselves bi-sexual. The conclusion shows that just over half of the respondents who participated with FSM after one year have same-sex attractions but do not consider themselves homosexual or gay.

16. **If you came to FSM having another form(s) of sexual or relational brokenness, how would you state your struggle?**
    Comment Box Used

Number of Sexual:	55
Number of Rational:	26
Number of N/A:	10
Number of Blank:	94
Sample Size = 185	

SQ-16
Table

A 5 percent sample of the total comments from SQ-16: Sexual and Relational (for all comments, see full published report).
Sexual:
- "A homo-sex addict"
- "Acted out sexually with multiple partners due to abuse and confused feelings."
- "Addicted to Internet pornography, infidelity, idol worship, sexually abused and abuser. Predator of women."
- "I considered myself homosexual but in agreement with Scripture that it was not a true description for a Christian even though I had SSA. My struggle with pornography (online) and the repugnance I felt about it is what caused me to contact FSM. I also was abused sexually as a child by an approx. six years older child/pre-teen."

Relational:

- "Because of my past, I didn't trust anyone. I got scared around other people and made problems for me in a lot of aspects in my life with relating to others."
- "Came to FSM because of unforgiveness in my heart towards a church that kicked me out for being a lesbian."
- "Emotional dependency"
- "I felt harassed by homosexual thoughts that I didn't want in my mind."

Question 16 Conclusion: For brevity, the details of this question were omitted. However, they can be reviewed in the full published report of the FSM Effectiveness Survey available at the First Stone website (www.firststone.org).

A 5 percent sample of the comments are below. 30 percent of all of the respondents answered their struggle was sexual. 14 percent of all the respondents answered that their struggle was relational. The majority of the entire survey, 56 percent did not answer SQ-16.

17. **Concerning being sexually abused.**

    Any act of sexual power (overt or covert) that is forced upon a child under eighteen years old. Abuse encompasses any form of sexual power directed at children from adults. That includes genital contact as well as sexual intention, e.g., leering and verbalized desire. Answered: The age of my first incidence of sexual abuse. Approximate number of times I was abused.

The age of my first incidence of sexual abuse — (55% Sexually Abused; 47% Sexually Abused older than 3 years.) — SQ-17

Answered: 166 Skipped: 19	Birth to 3 years	4 to 5 years	6 to 8 years	9 to 12 years	13 to 16 years	older than 16 years	N/A	Response Count
	8%	14%	14%	11%	6%	2%	45%	100%
About Me	14	23	24	18	10	3	74	166

Approximate number of times I was abused — (40% Sexually Abused at least 2 times; 33% Sexually Abused 3 or more times.)

Answered: 166 Skipped: 19	1 time	2 times	3-5 times	6-10 times	more than 10 times	N/A	Response Count
	14%	7%	13%	5%	14%	46%	100%
About Me	23	12	21	9	24	77	166

Were You Sexually Abused? & Did You Come to FSM Having Same-Sex Attractions? & Received Ministry for One or More Years & Sought Ministry for Self

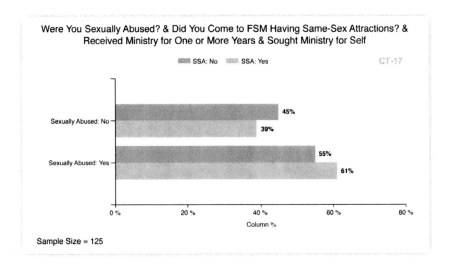

Sample Size = 125

Were You Sexually Abused? & Did You Come to FSM Having Same-Sex Attractions? & Received Ministry for One or More Years & Sought Ministry for Self

	Total	SSA: Yes	SSA: No
Sample Size	125	96	29
Sexually Abused: Yes			
Count	75	59	16
Column %	60%	61%	55%
Sexually Abused: No			
Count	50	37	13
Column %	40%	39%	45%

Concerning being sexually abused SQ-17 pertaining to SQ-15:

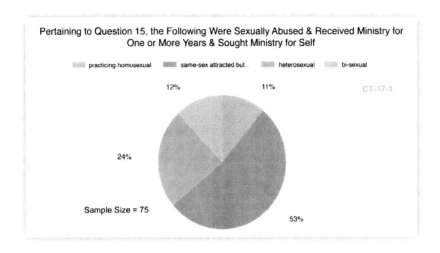

Pertaining to Question 15, the Following Were Sexually Abused & Received Ministry for One or More Years & Sought Ministry for Self

practicing homosexual   same-sex attracted but...   heterosexual   bi-sexual

12%   11%   CT-17-1

24%

Sample Size = 75

53%

Pertaining to Question 15, the Following Were Sexually Abused & Received Ministry for One or More Years & Sought Ministry for Self	Abused
Sample Size	75
practicing homosexual	
Count	8
Column %	11%
same-sex attracted but not homosexual	
Count	40
Column %	53%
heterosexual	
Count	18
Column %	24%
bi-sexual	
Count	9
Column %	12%

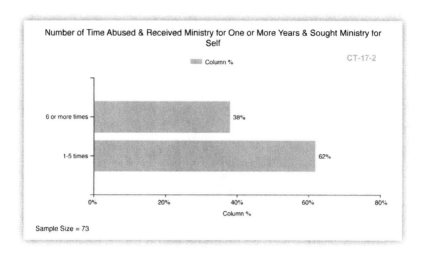

Number of Time Abused & Received Ministry for One or More Years & Sought Ministry for Self

	Total
Sample Size	73
1-5 times	
Count	45
Column %	62%
6 or more times	
Count	28
Column %	38%

Question 17 Conclusion: Out of the 185 survey respondents, 166 answered this question. 55 percent of the 166 respondents were sexually abused. From this group, 47 percent were sexually abused for more than three years. 40 percent were sexually abused at least twice, 33 percent were sexually abused more than three times. Of those who received

ministry for more than one year and sought help for themselves, 61 percent of those who were same-sex attracted were sexually abused. 11 percent of respondents who were sexually abused were practicing homosexuals, 53 percent experienced same-sex attractions, and 12 percent considered themselves bi-sexuals. 76 percent of those who sought help for themselves and participated with FSM for at least one year were sexually abused. Of this 76 percent main focus group, 100 percent were sexually abused several times and reported same-sex attractions.

Current Beliefs
18. Do you currently have same-sex attractions?
    a. Yes
    b. No
    c. N/A

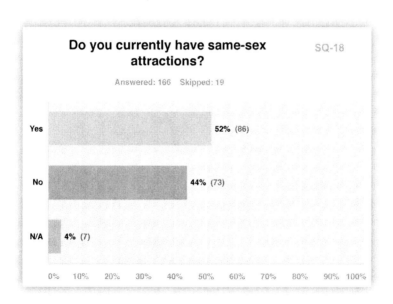

Do you currently have same-sex attractions?   SQ-18

Answered: 166   Skipped: 19

Yes   52% (86)
No   44% (73)
N/A   4% (7)

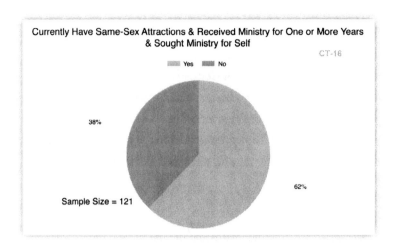

Currently Have Same-Sex Attractions & Received Ministry for One or More Years & Sought Ministry for Self			
	Yes	**No**	**Total**
Count	75	46	121
Row%	62%	38%	100%

Question 18 Conclusion: Of 185 respondents to SQ-18, 166 answered the question. 52 percent currently still have same-sex attractions. Of those who received ministry for one or more years and sought help for themselves, according to CT-18, the number of those who continue to have same-sex attraction was 62 percent.

19. If you do have same-sex attractions, do you currently consider yourself gay or homosexual?

a. Yes

b. No

c. N/A

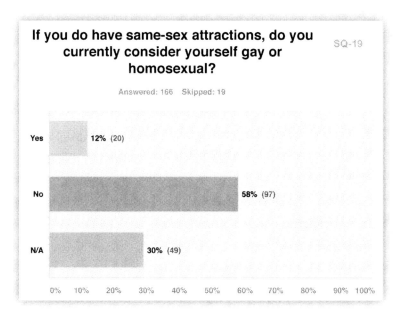

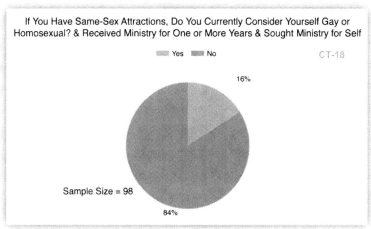

If You Have Same-Sex Attractions, Do You Currently Consider Yourself Gay or Homosexual? & Received Ministry for One or More Years & Sought Ministry for Self			
	Yes	No	Total
Count	16	82	98
Row %	16%	84%	100%

Question 19 Conclusion: Of the same 166 respondents, those who responded to SQ-18 report having same-sex attractions, however only 12 percent considered themselves practicing homosexuals or gay. Of those who have same-sex attractions and received ministry for one or more years and sought help for themselves, 84 percent do not consider themselves gay or homosexual after having been involved with FSM.

20. **Do you believe it is acceptable to God for you to behave in homosexual sexual acts?**
    a. Yes
    b. No

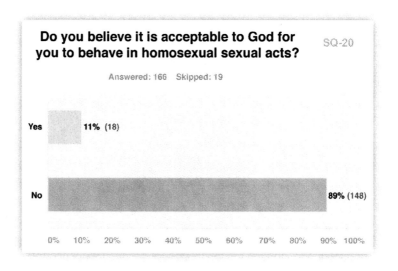

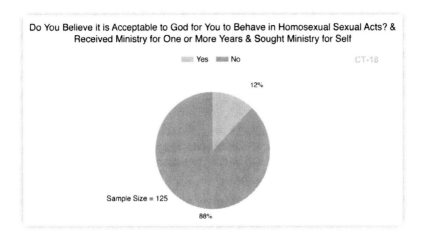

Do You Believe it is Acceptable to God for You to Behave in Homosexual Sexual Acts? &
Received Ministry for One or More Years & Sought Ministry for Self

Sample Size = 125

Do You Believe it is Acceptable to God for You to Behave in Homosexual Sexual Acts? & Received Ministry for One or More Years & Sought Ministry for Self			
	Yes	**No**	**Total**
Count	15	110	125
Row %	12%	88%	100%

Question 20 Conclusion: SQ-20 clearly reveals that the majority, 89 percent of respondents, do not believe homosexual behavior is acceptable to God. CT-20 only reveals a 1 percent difference of 88 percent after involvement with FSM. The conclusion is that the majority of those who come through FSM do not believe homosexual behavior is acceptable to God. This should not surprise anyone. The majority of the people who seek help from ministries such as First Stone are usually identified as Christians already. From SQ-5, 94 percent (of CT-5) respondents indicated that they were Christians.

21. Did FSM help you in overcoming any form of sexual sin and/or brokenness?

a. N/A

b. No

c. Yes (please explain what brokenness was overcome)

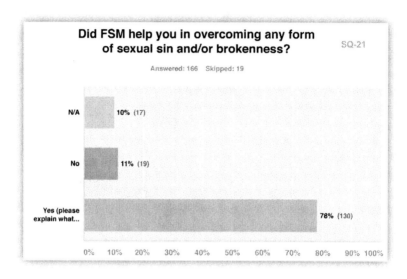

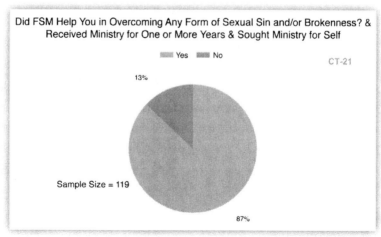

Did FSM Help You in Overcoming Any Form of Sexual Sin and/or Brokenness? & Received Ministry for One or More Years & Sought Ministry for Self			
	Yes	**No**	**Total**
Count	104	15	119
Row %	87%	13%	100%

A 5 percent sample of the total comments from SQ-21: Sins/ Brokenness Overcome Comments (for all comments, see full published report)—(please explain what brokenness was overcome)

- A great degree of victory over pornographic addiction, understanding and healing of emotional pain mentioned above with Jesus' help and truth.
- Addiction to pornography.
- "FSM + my church helped [me] overcome acting out sexually with other men."
- "Although I still have attractions to men, I now believe wholeheartedly that those desires are sinful to act upon. I have to ask the Lord daily for help with lust of the eyes. I am now in a heterosexual marriage and believe I am still being made holy daily by the Lord."
- "There were a number of things dealt with during the teaching and worship times. One that was significant to me was confronting my parents. It went really well, and I am grateful."
- "Yes! FSM really helped me to learn to forgive wholeheartedly the people who abused me as a child. I was coming out of a traumatic experience when I began there, and the help was extremely beneficial to my growth and well-being. The molestation was something that I healed greatly from and knowing that I was not being put down for my feelings but learning to deal with them in a more positive way was something I learned."

Question 21 Conclusion: SQ-21 had 159 respondents. Of these respondents, 78 percent believe FSM helped them overcome sexual sin and brokenness. CT-21 reveals 87 percent were helped in overcoming sexual sin and brokenness. The conclusion is overwhelming that FSM has been effective in helping people overcome sexual sin and brokenness, especially for those who came seeking help for themselves and who participated in the ministry for one or more years.

For the next few questions, please respond keeping in mind the following statements:

- *I believe I am currently living my life in accordance and in agreement with a biblically-orthodox worldview pertaining to human sexuality.*
- *Therefore, I believe in God's divine intent for human sexuality that is prescribed in the Holy Scriptures.*
- *I believe that marriage is only one man and one woman in a covenant until death separates them.*

22. **Select all that apply concerning the above statements:**
    a. I have never been married, but I agree with the preceding statement.
    b. I am married to the opposite sex, and I agree with the preceding statement.
    c. I was once married to the opposite sex, and I agree with the preceding statement.
    d. I cannot agree with the preceding statement.
    e. If Yes, are you married to the opposite sex now?

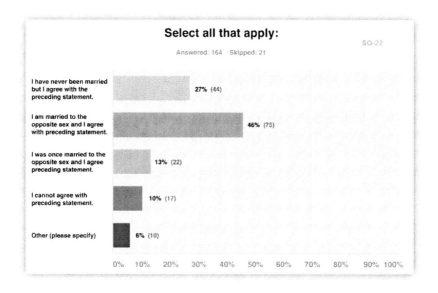

Select all that apply:

Answered: 164   Skipped: 21

SQ-22

I have never been married but I agree with the preceding statement.	27% (44)
I am married to the opposite sex and I agree with preceding statement.	46% (75)
I was once married to the opposite sex and I agree preceding statement.	13% (22)
I cannot agree with preceding statement.	10% (17)
Other (please specify)	6% (10)

0%   10%   20%   30%   40%   50%   60%   70%   80%   90%   100%

Other: (10 comments)

- "agree with statements 2 & 3."
- "I believe in the above but one person cannot hold a marriage together."
- "I believe that Jesus Christ is my Lord and Savior and accepts me as a homosexual"
- "I believe the Bible affords divorce for adultery."
- "I cannot form an opinion on the above statements at this time."
- "I don't believe God is damning people for broken sexual expression. I believe Jesus was the expression of the heart of God toward sin. He forgave us and accepting forgiveness produces repentance."
- "I have been happily married to person of the same sex for five years. [male w/male]."
- "I would like to be married one day and agree with the statements."
- "Still having problems with sexual sin, so I cannot agree with the first statement; the other two I can agree with."
- "Widowed and agree."

Question 22 Conclusion: SQ-22 reveals overwhelmingly that the majority, 86 percent of 164 respondents, believe that marriage should be between one man and one woman. 10 percent believe otherwise, embracing homosexual "marriage."

23. **If you were married or are married to the opposite sex, was this as a result of receiving pastoral care with FSM?**
    a. Yes
    b. No
    c. N/A

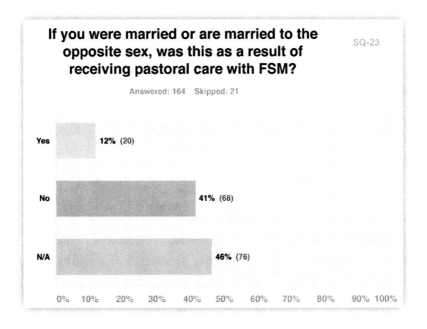

Question 23 Conclusion: 164 answered this question: 12 percent are married to the opposite sex as a result of their pastoral care at FSM.

24. Would you consider yourself a Christian maturing in your obedience and faith?

a. Yes
b. No

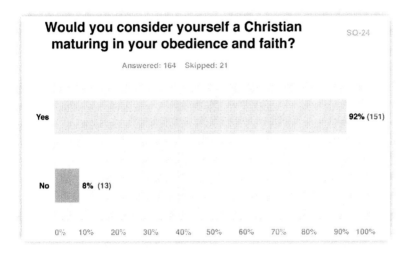

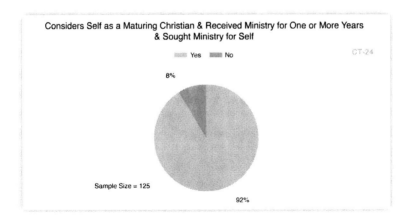

Considers Self as a Maturing Christian & Received Ministry for One or More Years & Sought Ministry for Self

	Yes	No	Total
Count	115	10	125
Row %	92%	8%	100%

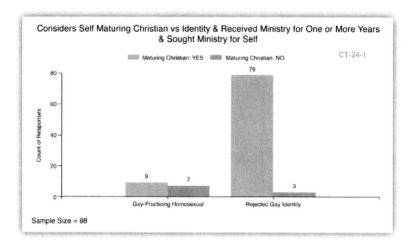

Considers Self Maturing Christian vs Identity & Received Ministry for One or More Years & Sought Ministry for Self

CT-24-1

Sample Size = 98

Considers Self Maturing Christian vs Identity & Received Ministry for One or More Years & Sought Ministry for Self

		Maturing Christian	
	Total	YES	NO
Sample Size	98	88	10
Homosexual			
Count	16	9	7
Column %	16%	10%	70%
Rejected Gay Identity			
Count	82	79	3
Column %	84%	90%	30%

Question 24 Conclusion: 92 percent of those who answered the question believe they are maturing Christians. Of the main focus group (CT-24), 94 percent believe they are maturing Christians. CT-24-1 shows the responses filtered by those who are gay-identified or practicing homosexual. There were nine respondents (10 percent) who identify themselves as gay or practicing homosexual *and* a maturing Christian. The majority of respondents, 90 percent, call themselves maturing Christians who reject a gay-identity or homosexual behavior.

25. **Would you consider yourself free from sexual addiction or sexual sin as a result of being involved with FSM?**
    a. Yes
    b. No
    c. N/A

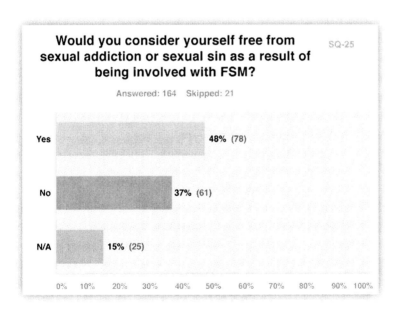

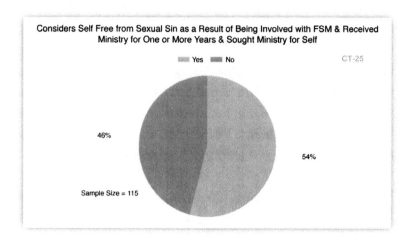

Considers Self Free from Sexual Sin as a Result of Being Involved with FSM & Received Ministry for One or More Years & Sought Ministry for Self			
	Yes	**No**	**Total**
Count	62	53	115
Row %	54%	46%	100%

Question 25 Conclusion: Of the 115 respondents, seventy-eight (or 67 percent) consider themselves free from sexual sin and brokenness as a result of their work with FSM. Sixty-two respondents (or 54 percent) said that after at least one year of ministry and seeking help for themselves, they considered themselves free from sexual sin and addiction. The next question reveals an additional 10 percent were free or mostly free, bringing the total closer to 77 percent.

26. If your answer to Question 25 is No, please select the best answer?

a. N/A

b. I already considered myself free.

c. I still consider myself addicted.

d. Other (please specify)

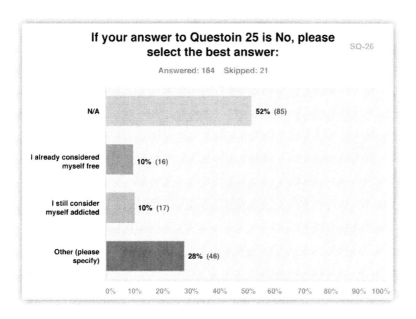

Other (please specify)		SQ-26 Table
Number Free:	10	5%
Number Mostly Free:	9	5%
Number Struggling:	17	9%
Number Gay:	4	2%
Number No Change:	2	1%
Number N/A:	3	2%
Number of Blank:	140	76%
Sample Size = 185		100%

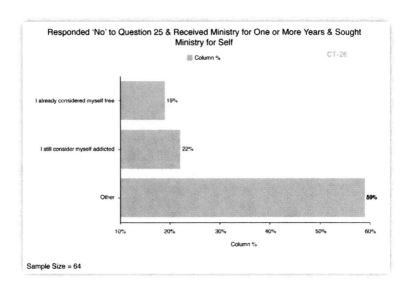

Responded 'No' to Question 25 & Received Ministry for One or More Years & Sought Ministry for Self	
	Total
Sample Size	64
I already considered myself free	
Count	12
Column %	19%
I still consider myself addicted	
Count	14
Column %	22%
Other	
Count	38
Column %	59%

Question 26 Conclusion: SQ-25 and SQ-26 percentages clearly reveal that 77 percent of respondents considered themselves free or mostly free from sexual addiction. The numbers demonstrate that FSM and related ministries (such as the Restored Hope Network) are effective in helping people overcome same-sex sexual addiction. CT-26 shows the smaller sample of 64 respondents (59 percent) who responded as "other". The "other" category break down is shown in the SQ-26 table.

27. **On the following scale, please rate your state of mind *BEFORE* you came to FSM.**
    a. Addicted
    b. Some Progress
    c. Mostly Free
    d. Free from Addiction
    e. N/A

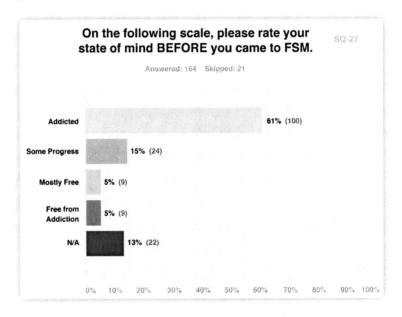

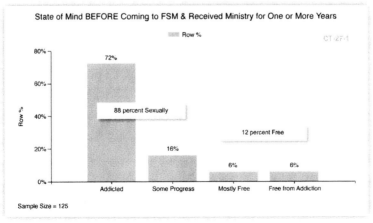

State of Mind BEFORE Coming to FSM & Received Ministry for One or More Years

	Addicted	Some Progress	Mostly Free	Free from Addiction	Total
Count	90	20	7	8	125
Row %	72%	16%	6%	6%	100%

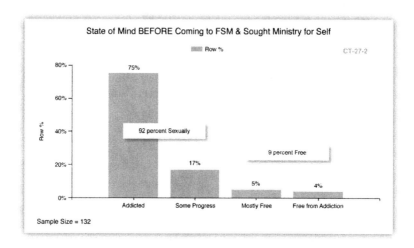

State of Mind BEFORE Coming to FSM & Sought Ministry for Self

	Addicted	Some Progress	Mostly Free	Free from Addiction	Total
Count	99	22	6	5	132
Row %	75%	17%	5%	4%	100%

Question 27 Conclusion: The overwhelming conclusion from SQ-27, CT-27-1 and CT-27-2 is that the majority of those who came to FSM were sexually broken. Of the main focus group, 88 percent to 92 percent considered themselves sexually broken. (CT 27-1 and CT-27-2).

28. **On the following scale, please rate your state of mind *AFTER* you left FSM.**
    a. Addicted
    b. Some Progress
    c. Mostly Free
    d. Free from Addiction
    e. N/A

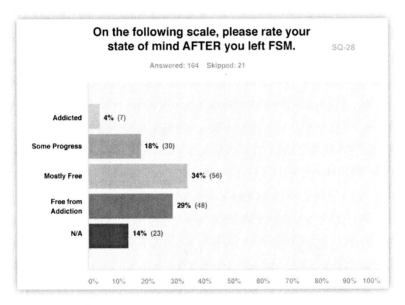

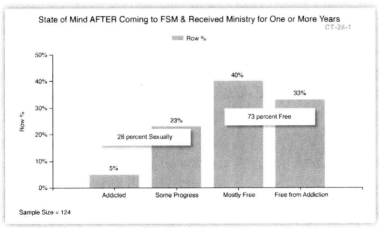

State of Mind AFTER Coming to FSM & Received Ministry for One or More Years

	Addicted	Some Progress	Mostly Free	Free from Addiction	Total
Count	6	28	49	41	124
Row %	5%	23%	40%	33%	100%

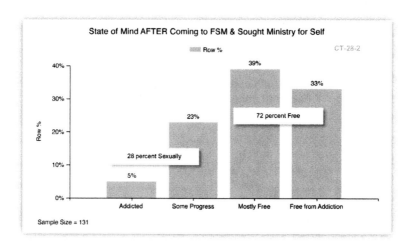

State of Mind AFTER Coming to FSM & Sought Ministry for Self

Sample Size = 131

State of Mind AFTER Coming to FSM & Sought Ministry for Self

	Addicted	Some Progress	Mostly Free	Free from Addiction	Total
Count	7	30	51	43	131
Row %	5%	23%	39%	33%	100%

Question 28 Conclusion: When the numbers from questions 27 and 28 are compared, we can conclude that ministries, such as First Stone, are effective in helping people overcome homosexuality, sexual addiction, and sexual brokenness. CT-28-1 and CT-28-2 clearly indicate that more than 72 percent found freedom by participating in First Stone Ministries for at least one year.

29. **Final Comments:**

Number of Yes:	85
Number of No:	7
Number of Mixed:	6
Number of N/A:	3
Number of Blank:	84
Sample Size = 185	

Question 29—Final Comments
5 percent sample of the final comments: Positive: Yes, No or Mixed
Yes:

- "Thanks again for all your help! The Lord has used you guys greatly in my life, helping me find freedom. I often remember the lesson on letting go of our labels. PTL [Praise the Lord] that I let go of the gay label!"
- "First Stone is a big, much needed ministry in OKC [Oklahoma City]. I cherish my friendships with FSM staff and support group members. We are friends for life. It was sad to see Exodus crash."
- "My time in ministry at FSM was a major turning point in my life. Through counseling I was set free from guilt I was carrying. Freed to hear more clearly from the Lord. I needed to work through some unhealthy relationships. Since then I have been more spiritually healthy, matured, and have been able to minister to others as I have walked in more freedom."
- "Thank you, FSM. You were a lifeboat for me when I really needed help. God bless your work and faithfulness to God. You are a continuing encouragement to me as I face my personal struggle with my flesh."
- "I am who I am today bc [because] of my years at FSM. I am so glad that I was led to meet with Brother Stephen before I met my

wife and was able to prepare myself for marriage being able to share my journey to freedom with her. I am still a work in progress but know that I am loved by God and strive to see myself as He does. Thank you, FSM!"

No:
- "My sincere hope is that ministries like this one cease and that abusive teachings will no longer be accessible to those attending and that they can go live in freedom in the way God made them and embrace their natural God given sexuality and as such be freed in every way."
- "[Gay man] After leaving this ministry, I came to a close personal relationship with Jesus Christ. He lives and accepts me just as I am. My husband and I are honoring God by raising our children in a Christian home that gives them a true sense of a loving Savior. I pray others will leave this terrible 'ministry' and find the real Jesus! How can you keep this torture going when so many have denounced it?"

Mixed:
- "First Stone helped me not to hate myself and introduced me to Jesus. But I am still gay. That hasn't and won't change."
- "My state of mind before FSM was determination to be freed from homosexuality because I thought that's what I needed. My state of mind after FSM was pure confusion and then later realized that I don't have a problem; God has made me perfectly just the way I am. I can be a Christian and love and serve God AND be gay. I have nothing but total respect for what you all do but it was not the right thing for me. I can see how you can help some people with sexual brokenness, but I don't feel like just because someone is gay that they are sexually broken."

Final Conclusion of the First Stone Ministries Effectiveness Survey: Ex-gay Ministries Are Effective

Let's look at the focus group of individual respondents of the survey, which consisted of 185 respondents (focus group—CT 166 & 149). Those who completed the survey identified as, "looking for help for themselves." They had participated in the ministry for a minimum of one year. The subset of people in the cross tabs (CT) clearly suggests that there are many people of faith in the United States who are unhappy and uncomfortable with their same-sex attractions. The majority those who took the survey rightfully define homosexual behavior as sin, especially since most of the people who come to our ministry are Christians. Of this focus group, at least 72 percent have found lasting freedom from sinful behavior (CT-28-2). We see clearly from the numbers and comments that people are filled with joy and are very satisfied to have a devoted relationship with Jesus Christ as their Lord and are free from being identified as gay or homosexual. The evidence is clear that there is real hope for lasting change when the answers from question 27 and 28 are compared and reviewed.

In Anne Paulk's book, *Restoring Sexual Identity*, we learn that 81 percent of gay-identified women, lesbians (ex-gays) who diligently sought help, also found lasting freedom (pg. 256). It is certain that ministries such as First Stone and the now fifty-plus organization in the Restored Hope Network are effective in helping people overcome homosexuality, sexual addiction, and all forms of sexual brokenness. We can reasonably assume that RHN ministries who are similar to First Stone. and who offer the same or similar services, will have the good success rates.

> that there are many people of faith in the United States who are unhappy and uncomfortable with their same-sex attractions.

265

Based upon the survey results, we can calculate and reasonably assume that at least 70 percent of the 1,200 clients (840 people) who spent at least one year with our ministry and who struggled with unwanted same-sex attractions found lasting freedom.

We started this research with over 1,200 client folders from 1989-2015. This was twenty-five years of client folders, including 1,030 email address, 500 whom we were confident we could reach. The result was 185 solid responses by the close of the thirteen-month survey. Based upon the survey results, we can calculate and reasonably assume that at least 70 percent of the 1,200 clients (840 people) who spent at least one year with our ministry and who struggled with unwanted same-sex attractions found lasting freedom.

There are forty RHN ministries that reach out to those in need by use of similar methods in ministry services. If you were to assume they experienced a similar success rate with a comparable number of participants, then you can reasonably imagine numbers upwards of 33,000 people who have been equipped to sustain lasting results in sexual healing ministries. This would be a conservative number as the people who were involved in other Exodus ministries over the last forty years were not counted. When many other groups are considered, such as the additional sixty or more *Living Waters Support Groups* nationwide with general levels of participation at a rate of twenty to fifty people per year, a similar success rate may account for another 1200 to 3000 people per year. Multiply that by thirty years of ministry through *Living Waters*, and you can reasonably imagine some 36,000 to 90,000 people who are free from same-sex attraction and a life defined, dominated, and darkened by homosexuality.

These results do not take into account the many churches who help people find a lifestyle away from homosexuality. We know that in the United States, there are at least thirty million conservative Christian church attenders, slightly less than 10 percent of the population, with 38 percent who claim to regularly attend church.[1] For the sake of estimation, if 1 percent of the thirty million conservative Christians (300,000) consider themselves same-sex attracted and the church employs sound biblical teaching and methods to help them, we could estimate that at least 72 percent or more of those who seek help could successfully find freedom. This means tens of thousands of people have left homosexuality behind (approximately 216,000 people). My suspicion is that even this estimation is a gross underestimation of the reality. It is more likely that there are many more people free from a homosexual existence.

Therefore, it is reasonable to conclude that there are at least tens of thousands of people across the United States who have permanently left a homosexual or gay identity. Dr. Lisa Diamond, (a lesbian activist and co-editor-in-chief of the American Psychological Association *Handbook of Sexuality)* is correct.[2] Dr. Diamond purports that human sexuality is fluid. As I have noted before, no one is born gay. The reality is that many people make choices to do all kinds of things in sexual behavior. The facts are in, the failed leader of Exodus International, Alan Chambers does not have credibility or basis to communicate that 99.9 percent of homosexual people do not change. Yet gay activists and gay media are thrilled with Chambers' statement and his closure of Exodus. The data from this survey proves conclusively that the opposite is true in what Chambers and his gay allies report.

> it is reasonable to conclude that there are at least tens of thousands of people across the United States who have permanently left a homosexual or gay identity.

The many of us who have experienced lasting change through an intimate relationship with Jesus Christ already knew these things to be true. God's grace does not keep people in bondage to sin. God's grace is transformational, and this is especially true for sexual sin. He loves us too much to leave us in bondage to sin. "Let God be true and every man a liar" (Rom. 3:4).

Peer Review Notes:

In concluding the results of this survey, it must be reported that the results were shared with peers for their review. These were peers who held PhDs that offer therapeutic models for helping others, from their reviews, the following were observed:

- This survey cannot be concluded to be a scientific contribution on the homosexual reality in the United States. The survey data is a mixture of formative and summative evaluation; therefore, formative data helps in knowing if your program is working, but the summative questions give too much of a range and a mixture to be a concrete scientific contribution.

- This survey also did not have the necessary baseline of history and current data to be completely scientific. However, the survey is a healthy offering of what many ministries currently experience that give full services of pastoral care, teaching, and support group environments. You received a very good level of data to support a conclusion that most people who wanted help, found it. It would be futile to argue with the testimonies of the many.

- The data from this survey should be viewed in comparison to the *A Longitudinal Study of Attempted Religiously Mediated Sexual Orientation Change* by Jones and Yarhouse.[3] The range of experiential change in behavior and attractions vary greatly. However, the conclusion of both the FSM Effectiveness Survey and the Longitudinal Study reveal a range from 30 to 70 percent of people in these surveys/studies want to leave a gay-identified existence and are successful at doing so. Therefore, it is solid conclusion that there are many people who do not want to live a gay-identified life, who identify as Christian, and many do in fact live a lifestyle congruent to their faith existence, where their behavior has changed to be in committed heterosexual relationships or as single celibates.[4]

Endnotes:

1. *How Many Evangelicals Are There?* - Wheaton College—Institute for the Study of American Evangelicals http://www.wheaton.edu/ISAE/Defining-Evangelicalism/How-Many-Are-There.
2. *Sexual Fluidity—Understanding Women's Love and Desire by Dr. Lisa M. Diamond,* ISBN 978-0674032262, Harvard University Press, February 2008.
3. *Ex-Gays?: A Longitudinal Study of Attempted Religiously Mediated Sexual Orientation Change by Stanton L. Jones, and Mark A. Yarhouse* ISBN: 978-0830828463, Publisher: IVP Academic.
4. Peer Review Notes are from Dr. Christopher Rosik, Psychologist, Therapist and Director of Research for Link Care, and Christopher Doyle, MA, LPC, LCPC, Licensed Professional Counselor helping people find freedom from unwanted same-sex attractions.

12

–THE CONCLUSION–

Freedom Realized is a Life of Uncompromised Faith—
Exposing Deceptive Relativism

"Now faith is the substance of things hoped for,
the evidence of things not seen.—Heb. 11:1

For whatever is born of God overcomes the world.
And this is the victory that has overcome the world—our faith.
—1 John 5:4

But without faith it is impossible to please Him, for he who comes to God
must believe that He is, and that He is a rewarder of those who
diligently seek Him."—Heb. 11:6

I, STEPHEN BLACK, WRITE THIS final chapter with the concluding thought: *Freedom Realized, Finding Freedom from Homosexuality and Living a Life Free from Labels is summed up with "Freedom Realized is about a life of uncompromising faith."* My concluding challenge to you is to endure to the very end of your life with a **real,** sincere, uncompromising faith in the **power of God**. If I accomplished

271

nothing else, I beg you to **believe God and His Word for more** than what is currently communicated by "gay Christians" and their advocates! They are **not** telling you the truth!

Now, how do we receive anything from God? How did we start our relationship with God? How can we believe for something different for our lives—for actual change from God? The answer is simple and yet profound: it really is by faith. In this life, we receive everything God gives us by faith.

We have a relationship with a God we cannot see.[1] It takes faith to believe in something you cannot see.[2] We trust in promises given to us by God in the Holy Scriptures, found in the Bible as followers of Christ. We believe that God sent His Son Jesus to die on the cross for our sins. (John 3:16). Jesus' death is merely historical fact for some. However, for those who are truly born again, this belief and meditation brings about the transformation of the soul. Being **born again** is a rejuvenation—a changing—a transformation of the soul. We are saved by grace. Grace is the power of the Holy Spirit entering our mind, will, and emotions. This power directs us to a lifestyle of repentance. We are saved by grace through faith. This belief system is completely founded on the promises of God and what He accomplished through Jesus Christ. This is the foundation for our relationship with God, the Christian faith. This also is the foundation for the same-sex attracted struggler, the homosexual, or sex addicted. Freedom can only be realized by truly *"believing from the heart, resulting in righteousness."*[3]

A problem arises when a sincere faith is distorted by false messengers of grace. Jesus asked a powerful question about faith on earth at His return. *"...when the Son of Man comes, will He really find faith on earth?"* —Luke 18:8. To believe for everything that God has for us and to reach for holiness by faith is distorted today by those who struggle with same-sex attractions and advocates for so-called "gay Christianity." A poor theological perspective on faith leaves little room for the power of transformative grace. However, a fully consecrated heart embraces biblical truth in God's holy promises, and, *"believes from the heart, resulting in righteousness,"* and a changed life. Poor theology about faith minimizes the need to stay faithful to God, even if it means a lifetime of suffering in the flesh. Instead, there is a mix of the world's beliefs and psychology concerning homosexuality that gives way to unbelief. You either truly believe God, or you waver in unbelief. There are many who say that they believe God but do not trust Him for more, especially in helping to minimize unnatural same-sex desires over time.

The greatest enemy of a Christian is the attack on our faith in God, which is the spirit of unbelief. *All* sin can be identified as starting with unbelief. From Adam and Eve in the garden, who did not take seriously the promise and the warning of God, to modern day messengers of perverted grace, a false peace has been proclaimed and we are advised not to worry about the judgment to come on those who practice homosexuality. Unbelief is the heart condition that will not fully trust God's promises of blessing or the promises of judgment on certain behaviors. This unbelief empowers people to remain in darkness and conflicting identities that are completely contrary to God's promises found in the Holy Scriptures.

It is extremely important to understand that the promise of eternal life in Jesus Christ is synonymous with a life that walks in repentance, specifically in two areas. We see these two areas in commandments from Genesis to Revelation. These two areas are sexual immorality and idolatry. The Bible is clear and warns that those who practice these behaviors will be excluded from the kingdom of God. It cannot be any clearer. You will not go to heaven if you are an unrepentant, sexual idolater. When the apostles met together to decide what must be preached to keep the integrity of the Gospel message to the Gentiles, the Gospel of faith and not of works, they concluded that faith in Christ must produce a lifestyle free from sexual immorality and idolatry.[4] It was imperative that these two points of repentance from all forms of sexual immorality and idolatry

must be preached. *"If anyone teaches otherwise and does not consent or conform to wholesome words, even the words of our Lord Jesus Christ, and to the doctrine which accords with godliness, he is proud, knowing nothing, but is obsessed with disputes and arguments over words, from which come envy, strife, reviling, evil suspicions…" (1 Tim. 6:2-4).*

There are many today who lower the standards of faith. With a religious, mocking spirit, these people who call themselves "gay Christians" are subtly used by the devil to allow a demonic spirit of uncleanness to enter the church. They present themselves as victims. They present a message that does not require cleansing the inner-world of thinking, the mind, the emotions, and the will concerning same-sex attractions. They claim to be *"washed and waiting."* They call themselves washed in the blood of Jesus, yet they are waiting on God to do more. Until then, they teach that you must accept a lower standard by mixing being gay and Christianity. They also call themselves *"torn."* Some call themselves "celibate gay Christians." This deceives people with the claim that grace does not really change the inner-heart (the soul) of same-sex attracted people or former homosexuals. Some are even theologians and Bible teachers, yet they continue to perpetuate the deceived idea that you can mix a fallen construction of humanity in the distorted desires of the flesh's pursuits. They promote the unbelief that you can embrace same-sex attractions/lusts or inordinate desires of any kind with Christlikeness. They also promote the idea of a deep love (even romantic) between same-sex attracted people, *"spiritual friends"* because they are sexless relationships. Yet they also promote emotional idolatry and dependency as they nullify the need to outgrow same-sex attraction and become mature men and women in God.[5]

Please pause here and really think for a moment: the promotion in the church from these victim-minded "gay Christians" and their advocates ask church leaders to embrace a belief that God Almighty cannot, or will rarely, change a person's sexual attractions, desires, and lust. It is surprising how many scholarly teachers of the Word of God embrace this relativism in sinful unbelief by the promotion of "gay Christianity." I adamantly disagree with these highly academically and theologically educated people. In fact, they are truly uneducated in heaven's transformative power, and it seems, unknowingly mocking the Creator. I want to hope the best and believe they are unaware of how offensive this is to many surrendered Christians. They merge "gay" with Christlikeness as acceptable. It is truly offensive to the sincere ex-gays, who have known God's power to deliver, by their many years of faithful surrender to God's grace for change. It is grievous to many people, like me, who disdain labels of corruption, such as "gay." We also forsake any labels, including "ex-gay." The promotion of "gay Christianity" by so-called Christian leaders is very unloving to say the least and akin to being blasphemous putting homosexuality before Christ.

I am not talking about mere appreciation or assessment of the attractiveness of one's own gender. Big deal if you can identify someone of your own gender as attractive! Most of the men and women (ever-straights) in my world can find members of their own gender attractive. So what? No. This is not it. The *"washed and waiting"* the *"torn"* people and their advocates promote a dangerous and subtle attack on the faith of many because it subtly erodes the church's ability to believe for more and a subtle embracing of sexual uncleanness. There are many who advocate a once-prayed-always-saved mindset, which communicates that the celibate gay Christians are nothing to be concerned about because they are saved—a kind of a be-happy-don't-worry-philosophy. They are deceived. Beloved this is a huge problem. They lower God's standards and minimize the power available to us through Jesus Christ. They cry for authenticity and to be given space in the church. They call it "spacious graciousness." They ask to be accepted in the church without a desire for repentance or change of the internal desires and lusts for others. Authenticity is not a call to be true to the sinful nature. Biblical

> Authenticity is not a call to be true to the sinful nature. Biblical authenticity calls for a life lived in the light. True authenticity in God's economy produces humility, which in turn produces transformation.

authenticity calls for a life lived in the light. True authenticity in God's economy produces humility, which in turn produces transformation. Authenticity does not leave a soul in bondage to a same-sex attracted identity. True authenticity, born of faith in God, produces a new lifestyle of repentance and love. It leaves distorted labels of "gay" behind in the pit from which they came so as to embrace Christ as a new creation. (2 Cor. 5:17). I know about that evil pit. I have *no* stones to throw here, I merely advocate for real transparency and honesty—a holy life, which produces complete devotion to Jesus Christ and real change in the soul.

Many in the church create a problem of linking together the broken soul—the person driven with same-sex attractions and a lust-filled heart—with those mature believers who can merely experience attraction of one's gender. The latter is the maturing soul who remains consistently pure in heart and takes his thoughts captive concerning his past involvement with either homosexual fantasy (SSA lust) or actual behavior. The maturing Christian truly forsakes the false construct and the teaching of sinful humanity—that teaching that mixes homosexuality with Christlikeness as a "gay-Christian." The maturing person of God knows this is a war in the soul, mind, will, and emotions (2 Cor. 10:3-5). They rely on God's powerful grace to win the battles in the soul. God's grace, in consistent humility, (James 4:6), absolutely changes the inner world of saints who have struggled with homosexuality at any level.

No doubt, it will take a longer season of growth for those who had more wounding and years of sin in their lives, especially those who had embraced rebellion many times. Unfortunately, those who continue to sin, stumble and play with the evils of pornography and lust will not find freedom. Truly, the consequences are real and treacherous. Know confidently, that those who go back embracing a gay identity, did not stop the playing. We only walk in true freedom when we put away sin and die to self. We only walk in freedom if we have real integrity in the inner world of thinking and stop playing around. This is the *real,* relevant message in our day. It is not a new message, it is a *real,* biblically orthodox message of those who love the Word of God.

Several people from under the failed leadership of Alan Chambers in Exodus International and their new "gay Christian" friends, have concluded that real freedom over same-sex attraction/lust is not obtainable in this life. This says God is not powerful enough, and that they know better than God. They are truly under the gay *pride banner* of six colors as they continue to play. Ultimately, they are completely unaware in their lusts that this very banner of gay pride is a banner that asks for God's judgment. (Jude 1:7, 2 Peter 2:4-22, 2 Peter 3:10-16).

We cannot afford to embrace this distorted view of sanctification and lower our standards concerning the quest for lasting freedom and transformation. I am so grateful for the Restored Hope Network (RHN) leadership. I know many in RHN who stand strong and believe for much better as sincere believers in an uncompromising faith! They live lives of *real* faith! I also know many others who are not connected with any associations who walk in freedom and also live lives of *real* faith free from former same-sex attraction and lusts. These are godly men and women who believe that God's grace comes to transform the soul and the inner world of integrity concerning sexual desire and feelings! As these people have become known and open, the church is greatly helped and blessed by these people of integrity. These are my heroes!

We are in a fight for the truth in an uncompromising faith. Paul told Timothy our new life is called a fight of faith for a reason.[6] The wave of doubt and unbelief coming against the church concerning the transformation of people with same-sex attraction opens doors to demonic forces. Andrew Comiskey's message at the RHN Conference of 2016 entitled "Scandalous Good News," was a prophetic warning on the realities of faithful men and women leaving the labels of gay and ex-gay behind *will* be persecuted by those who embrace the "gay Christian" message.[7] It seems anyone who proclaims the message of real hope of freedom from same-sex attraction is scandalized.

I experienced a sad conflict here in the Oklahoma City church the week immediately following the prophetic word from Andrew in his "Scandalous Good News" message with a local church who embraced, "gay Christianity." We must remember that for the saints who have gone before us, the promises were not always obtained until after death when they entered heaven. Faithful Christians have always been scandalized and persecuted for believing for more. The mark of a real saint is perseverant hope for holiness. The persistent quest for transformation is the plumb-line of *real* faith in one's soul. We must hope and believe for better as we seek holiness in our thought-life. We must also be willing to suffer, believing that God does transform the souls of the same-sex attracted and the homosexual. True integrity in the inner-world of thought is obtainable! I do not speak of sinless perfection. I say only that to become maturing men and women made in the image of God, no exceptions for His divine intent for our genders and sexuality can be allowed. There must be no compromise on this matter! There are no same-sex attractions with lust and homosexuality in that image of God—in Imago Dei—with God's created humanity! Imago Dei is God's divine intent. Will you allow God to set you free and perfect His

> Will you allow God to set you free and perfect His divine image in your life, even if it means suffering until the end of your life?

divine image in your life, even if it means suffering until the end of your life? Will you forsake all false labels that only cause confusion and bondage? Will you live a life of belief in His promises and allow Him to name your identity and mold it from His Word? If you will, God promises that *"He who began this work in you will complete it."*—*Phil. 1:6.*

Endnotes:
1. 1 Peter 1:8-9
2. Heb. 11:1-6
3. John 3:16, Eph. 2:8-9, John 14:16-18, 26, John 15:26, John 16:7-13, 1 Cor. 2:13, Titus 2:11-14, Rom. 10:10
4. Acts 15:18-22, 21:25, Eph. 5:5-6, Rev. 21:6-8, 22:14-15
5. Wesley Hill, author of *Washed and Waiting: Reflections on Christian Fullness and Homosexuality,* and *Spiritual Friendship: Finding Love in the Church as a Celibate Gay Christian,* and Justin Lee Founder of The Gay Christian Network and author of *Torn: Rescuing the Gospel from the Gays-vs.-Christians Debate* (Neither book is recommended reading).
6. 1 Tim. 6:12
7. Scandalous Good News—by Andrew Comiskey—Find the text, audio, and video of this presentation at: http://www.firststone.org/articles/post/scandalous-good-news

13

MINISTRY HELPS

- First Stone Ministries—www.firststone.org
- Stephen Black—www.stephenblack.org
- Ministry Networks and Links—For a complete and up-to-date list of recommended ministries: www.firststone.org/helpful-links
- Restored Hope Network—(see find help) www.restoredhopenetwork.org—a national network of ministers dedicated in helping people find freedom from homosexuality, sexual sin, sexual addictions, and gender confusion.
- PFOX—www.pfox.org—a network of ministries helping families with gay identified children.
- Desert Stream Ministries—Living Waters—www.desertstream.org—an international ministry of support groups, resources, and leadership training.
- Taking Back Ground—Online Discipleship Program—www.takingbackground.com—an online program helping people in hard to reach places.

- Reach Truth—Online Map for Youth—www.reachtruth.com—an online resource for youth who desire help with unwanted same-sex attractions.
- Help 4 Families—www.help4families.com—ministry dedicated to the help and teaching on transgender and gender confusion.
- Genesis Counseling—Ministry of Joe Dallas—www.joedallas.com—counseling ministry and international speaker and teacher for gaining understanding all things in overcoming homosexuality.
- Overcomers Network—www.overcomersnetwork.org—a networking of ministries reaching the African American communities affirming change and freedom from homosexuality.
- Alliance for Therapeutic Choice—www.therapeuticchoice.com—a national network of therapists specializing in helping in the recovery of homosexuality and all underlying traumatic issues. (www.narth.com)
- Courage—www.couragerc.org—A Catholic twelve-step recovery group for overcoming homosexuality for men and women.
- Dr. Robert A. J. Gagnon—www.robgagnon.net—Greek scholar and professor of New Testament theology, a renowned expert on the biblical texts, hermeneutics, and the world history on the subject of homosexuality.
- Dr. Michael Brown—www.askdrbrown.org—international speaker, radio host, and author—an authority on biblical orthodox teaching on homosexuality.
- Dennis Jernigan—www.dennisjernigan.com—ex-gay international Psalmist and minister of music to bring healing to the soul, and freedom from homosexuality.

14

RECOMMENDED RESOURCES

UNDERSTANDING HOMOSEXUALITY
- **Counseling the Homosexual** - by Michael R. Saia
- **The Gay Gospel?*** - by Joe Dallas
- **Homosexuality and the Politics of Truth** - by Jeffery Satinover
- **The Bible and Homosexual Practice: Texts and Hermeneutics***
  - by Robert A. J. Gagnon
- **Open to Life*** - by Andrew Comiskey
- **Speaking of Homosexuality *** - by Joe Dallas

OVERCOMING HOMOSEXUALITY
GENERAL
- **The Broken Image**** - by Leanne Payne
- **Can You Be Gay and Christian?*** - by Michael L. Brown
- **Coming Out of Homosexuality** - by Bob Davies and Lori
- Rentzel
- **Coming Out Straight**** - by Richard Cohen, M.A.
- **Desires in Conflict*** - by Joe Dallas
- **Destiny Bridge*** - by Frank Worthen

- **Emotional Dependency** * - by Lori Thorkelson-Rentzel
- **First Steps Out of Homosexuality** * - by Frank Worthen
- **Hope for the Same-Sex Attracted** * - by Ron Citlau
- **Love Hunger** - by David Kyle Foster
- **Pursuing Sexual Wholeness** * - by Andrew Comiskey
- **Renewing Your Mind** *—by Dennis Jernigan
- **Setting Love in Order** - by Mario Bergner
- **Sexual Healing, God's Plan for the Sanctification of Our**
- **Lives** * - by David Kyle Foster
- **Sing Over Me: An Autobiography (Freedom from Homosexuality)** - by Dennis Jernigan
- **Strength in Weakness: Healing Relational and Sexual Brokenness** * - by Andy Comiskey
- **You Don't Have to Be Gay** * - by Jeff Konrad

FOR WOMEN
- **Called Out** - by Janet Boynes
- **Into the Promised Land** - by Jeanette Howard
- **Out of Egypt** - by Jeanette Howard
- **Restoring Sexual Identity** * - by Anne Paulk

FOR YOUTH / YOUNG ADULTS
- **Reach Truth** * - Online program twenty weeks in length. www.reachtruth.com
- **Soulutions** * - Study guide by Cathy Morrill

RELATIONAL & SPIRITUAL WHOLENESS IN GENERAL
- **Bondage Breaker** * - by Neil T. Anderson
- **Boundaries** * - Dr. Henry Cloud and Dr. John Townsend
- **Boundaries in Dating** - Dr. Henry Cloud and Dr. John Townsend

- **Boy Meets Girl: Say Hello to Courtship**** - by Joshua Harris
- **Breaking Free from the Spirit of Death** - by Jonathan Hunter
- **Clearing the Land*** - by Geri McGhee
- **Dating vs Courtship** - by Paul Jehle
- **False Intimacy** - by Harry W. Schaumburg
- **Hyper-Grace*** - by Michael L. Brown
- **I Kissed Dating Goodbye**** - by Joshua Harris
- **The Father Heart of God** - by Floyd McClung, Jr.
- **The Mom Factor*** - by Dr. Cloud and Dr. Townsend
- **Safe People*** - by Dr. Cloud and Dr. Townsend
- **Strength in Weakness: Healing Relational and Sexual Brokenness*** - by Andy Comiskey
- **Transformed into His Image***- David Kyle Foster
- **Victory over Darkness*** - by Neil T. Anderson
- **What's the Difference?*** **- Manhood and Womanhood**
- **Defined** - by John Piper

FOR MEN
- **Crisis In Masculinity**** - by Leanne Payne
- **Growth into Manhood: Resuming the Journey** ** - by Alan Medinger
- **Every Man's Battle**** - by Arterburn and Stoker
- **Falling Forward*** - Study guide by Craig Lockwood (Sex Addicts)
- **Wild at Heart*** - by John Eldredge

FOR WOMEN
- **The Friendships of Women** - by Dee Brestin
- **Sex and the Soul of a Woman*** - by Paula Rinehart
- **Strong Women, Soft Hearts*** - by Paula Rinehart

SEXUAL ABUSE / BROKENNESS

- **Naked Surrender*** - by Andrew Comiskey
- **Sexual Offending and Restoration**** - by Mark Yantzi
- **The Wounded Heart, Hope for Adult Victims of Sexual Abuse*** - by Dr. Dan B. Allender
- **The Wounded Spirit** - by Frank Peretti

PARENTS / FAMILY

- **A Parent's Guide to Preventing Homosexuality** - by Dr. & Mrs. Nicolosi
- **Bringing Up Boys*** - by James Dobson, PH.D
- **Dancing in the Arms of God*** - by Connie Neal (For Wives)
- **Hope for the Same-Sex Attracted*** - by Ron Citlau
- **Parents in Pain*** - by John White
- **Reaching Your Prodigal*** - by Phil Waldrep (Feb 2016)
- **Parenting Prodigals CD*** - by Phil Waldrep
- **Praying Your Prodigal Home*** - by Richard A. Burr
- **Shattered Dreams*** - by Larry Crabb
- **Someone I Love Is Gay*** - by Anita Worthen and Bob Davies
- **Speaking of Homosexuality*** - by Joe Dallas
- **The Best You Can Ever Give Your Parents** - by Dennis Rainey, Dave Boehi
- **The Tribute and the Promise*** - by Dennis Rainey, Dave Boehi
- **What's a Father to Do?** - by Don Schmierer
- **When Homosexuality Hits Home*** - by Joe Dallas

SPOUSES / MARRIAGE RELATED TO HOMOSEXUALITY

- **Where Do I Go from Here?** - by Annette Comiskey

MARRIED / PREMARITAL COUPLES

- **A Lasting Promise** - by Scott M. Stanley, Daniel Trathen, Savanna McCain and Milt Bryan
- **For Men Only: A Straightforward Guide to the Inner Lives of Women*** - by Shaunti & Jeff Feldhahn
- **For Women Only: What You Need to Know about the Inner Lives of Men** - by Shaunti Feldhahn
- **His Needs, Her Needs*** - by Dr. Willard Harley
- **Love Dare*** - by Stephen & Alex Kenrick
- **Love Life for Every Married Couple*** - by Dr. Ed Wheat and Gloria Okes Perkins
- **Love & Respect*** - by Dr. Emerson Eggerichs
- **Preparing for Marriage*** - by David Boehi, Brent Nelson, Jeff Schulte and Lloyd Shadrach
- **Saving Your Marriage Before It Starts** - by Drs. Les & Leslie Parrott

SEX IN MARRIAGE

- **The Gift of Sex**** - by Clifford & Joyce Penner
- **Intended for Pleasure****- by Ed Wheat

VIDEOS

- **PurePassion Season 8*** - DVD (Over 500 PurePassion Online Videos located: http://www.cross.tv/profile/175377)*
- **Reconciliation Movie*** - DVD
- **Such Were Some of You*** - DVD
- **How Do You Like Me Now*** - DVD
- **Tranzformed*** - DVD

SUGGESTED ONLINE SITES*

- firststone.org
- restoredhopenetwork.org
- desertstream.org
- robgagnon.net
- joedallas.com
- narth.com
- settingcaptivesfree.com
- andrewcomiskey.org
- covenanteyes.com
- dennisjernigan.com
- help4families.com
- pfox.org
- purepassion.us
- pureintimacy.org
- suchweresomeofyou.org
- howdoyoulikemenow.org
- tranzformed.org

* *Highly Recommended by First Stone Ministries
(Read/Watched and Endorsed by Stephen Black)*
** *First Stone Ministries/ Stephen Black does not necessarily endorse
all the concepts/teachings OR contributors presented.*

ORDER INFORMATION

To order additional copies of this book, please visit
www.redemption-press.com.
Also available on Amazon.com and BarnesandNoble.com
Or by calling toll free 1-844-2REDEEM.

CPSIA information can be obtained
at www.ICGtesting.com
Printed in the USA
FFOW05n0832071017